The Kogan Page Market Resea[r]ch [...] market research publishing. W[...] embracing tomes covering every [...] title in this new series is devote[d] [...] area.

The prime aim of the titles in the series is to demystify the technicalities of market research by providing concise, digestible introductions, presented in a clear and comprehensive style.

Well-illustrated throughout, these practical guides will serve as vital introductions for those new to market research, useful revision tools for students and essential refreshers for all market research professionals.

Titles in the series are:

Questionnaire Design
Interviewing
Sampling and Statistics
Desk Research
Buying Market Research

ABOUT THE AUTHORS

■

Paul Hague is a Chairman of Business & Market Research plc. He regularly contributes to the market research trade press and lectures at seminars on the subject. He is author of *The Industrial Market Research Handbook* and co-author of *Do Your Own Market Research, How to do Marketing Research* and *Market Research in Practice*. In addition to this, he co-authored three other books in the Market Research Series — *Questionnaire Design, Interviewing* and *Sampling and Statistics* with Paul Harris. He is also joint editor of *A Handbook of Market Research Techniques*. All these books are published by Kogan Page.

Kate Roberts started her career at Waddingtons working in their export sales and marketing division, which included a period managing its French operation. She then went on to become a director of Business & Market Research plc, and now works alongside Paul Hague in industrial and business-to-business research.

PRESENTATIONS AND REPORT WRITING

Paul Hague and Kate Roberts

KOGAN
PAGE

First published in 1994

Kogan Page Limited
120 Pentonville Road
London N1 9JN

© Paul Hague and Kate Roberts, 1994

British Library Cataloguing in Publication Data

A CIP record for this book is available from the British Library.

ISBN 0 7494 1227 5

Typeset by BookEns Limited, Baldock, Herts.
Printed and bound in Great Britain by Biddles Ltd, Guildford and Kings Lynn.

CONTENTS

■

Presentations

PREFACE

■

It seems to us that market research is much undervalued in the business world. Within the field of business consultancy, market research sits very much on the fringe while the management consultants take the high ground. Market researchers have no one to blame but themselves. What they do is vital to the running of all businesses, for who would dispute the need for sound information to guide the decision-making process? The quality of the information which market researchers obtain is seldom in question. Where they fall down is in communicating to their clients what they have found out in a clear, simple and authoritative manner.

No one commissions market research for its own sake. It always has a purpose and should always justify its cost. This may not be evident if the information is badly presented, cluttered and with no obvious conclusion. The presentation of the findings of market research, whether in the written or spoken word, is *the* most important part of the researcher's work. It is the embodiment of the project. The written report is a permanent record of what has been found out, while the personal presentation offers the chance for the researcher to stamp personality on the project and to stimulate, as well as educate, the audience. Both the report and the presentation are opportunities for market researchers to make themselves noticed, not as boring, heads-in-the-cloud academics, but people who have an important role to play in helping shape business decisions.

Writing reports and making effective presentations are the most difficult parts of the market researcher's task. Many people take years to get it right. This is not because report writing and presentations are difficult, it is because researchers lack confidence. Confidence comes out of a sense of authority; a realisation of what is required and how to deliver it. For many people in market research the appointment is at the beginning of their career. They are in their early twenties and though confident in many aspects of life, answering to a room full of experienced managers is daunting.

This book aims to help researchers improve their confidence in report writing and presentations by showing how to communicate clear, interesting and instructive information. Our aim is to provide guidelines and tips which will result in immediate improvements. More than this we hope it encourages readers to do the most important thing of all, which is to take every opportunity to write reports and present findings because it is only through doing so that the skills will be developed and confidence achieved.

Paul Hague
Kate Roberts
May 1994

INTRODUCTION

∎

THE PURPOSE OF REPORTS AND PRESENTATIONS

The main purpose of a market research report is to communicate the findings of the survey as clearly as possible to other people. These 'other people' could be colleagues within the same company (in-house clients) or paying clients of a market research agency.

There are two ways of communicating the findings to the client: a written report and a verbal presentation. In most projects both are required. In most cases the norm is to present the results in person and follow up the verbal presentation with a written report. For some clients the report is almost superfluous and a paper copy of the presentation charts is sufficient for their needs. However, others will want a written report for the following reasons:

■ As a permanent reference document. Long after everyone has forgotten the presentation and the exact details of what was done and why, the report can be referred to for clarification.

■ To allow circulation of the research findings to a wider audience. A director may not have the time to attend a presentation but still wants to be informed of the outcome of the research.

■ To provide a comprehensive record of the research

project. A presentation may only cover the key findings, whereas a written report provides a detailed record of the research.

UNDERESTIMATED SKILLS

Surely there is nothing to writing reports and making presentations? Our education process teaches us how to write and by the time we are in our early twenties we have learned good communicative skills, so what is all the fuss about report writing and presentation? Only when you have to do it does the realisation sink in. Writing the report is an agony. It seems impossible to get the right words together and the whole thing is disjointed. The first time you have to make a presentation you meet reality with a bang and find out that your mind and body seem to be confused and the words you wanted to say do not come out as you had hoped, you are nervous, you feel faint and the whole event is an unpleasant experience.

You feel undermined by the media. Every time you pick up the paper there is a well-written analysis of something or other; the television contains one presentation after another from the news to chat shows: a whole series of people are talking clearly and confidently, making it look so easy. Why is it then that writing market research reports and giving presentations of market research findings prove so difficult?

REPORT WRITING AND PRESENTATIONS ARE NOT EASY

The first difficulty researchers face is that report writing and presentations are not like anything they have ever done before. A market research report is not like the essays that were written at school or university. Reports record and communicate findings that have probably come from many different sources. They need a structure and a writing style quite different to that used in other fields. Market research presentations are quite different to anything else. They are neither after dinner speeches, nor debates nor discussions with friends. Just as market research reports are special in their own way, so too market research presentations have their own structure and style.

The second difficulty faced by the novice researcher is the pressure that is engendered by the scale of the project. Market research projects often have price tags at least equal to those of a car. Expectations are high since the cost is considerable. The reports and presentations are not examined formally but every part of the project is scrutinised by some audience or another. Many within the audience will be senior in status and this creates an immense pressure on the researcher who may suffer from self-doubt and a feeling of a lack of credibility.

In the same way that restaurants are judged by their last meal, so too market researchers are judged on their last report or presentation. One bad examination paper can be compensated for by others that are good but a poor report or presentation may be remembered for a long time. The researcher is writing the report or giving the presentation alone but represents a company or a team who helped in its compilation. If the project is deemed a failure, there is the pressure of admitting this to colleagues back at the office.

The third and final difficulty with many market research reports and presentations is that the subject area is not easy. Market research is often commissioned to solve difficult business decisions. If the research is wrong, jobs and investments could be at stake. The answers arising from the research may not be clear. A whole new stack of questions may be posed at the end of the research which could not have been anticipated at the start — or could they? Researchers by their very nature want to get the answer right. They are so steeped in the subject of data collection and analysis that they sometimes forget that someone, somewhere will need to make a decision, and beating about the bush will not help. There is always too little time and not enough resource to do a good job but that is no excuse for prevarication.

Raising the difficulties of writing reports and making presentations is not intended to put the researcher off, rather it is to point out that everyone struggles with these two issues and this is to be expected. Reassuringly, the craft of report writing and presentation can be learned and very often it is just a matter of practice and applying a number of tips.

DEALING WITH DEADLINES

All market research projects have a timetable with a date for completion, which becomes the driver from the outset. The report and the presentation come at the very end of the project and so they are squeezed if things fall behind schedule. There are numerous reasons why projects can fall behind — not all of them the researcher's fault. The research sponsor may take a long time to check over the questionnaire. Bad weather could slow down the interviewing. A computer failure could result in lost data. These excuses do not help if the date for the report and presentation is cast in stone. As a result, the researcher may have to write a report in a shorter space of time than would be ideal, often late into the evening or over a weekend.

It is not always a delay in the research process that pressurises the report writing. Some people simply cannot motivate themselves until the last minute. It is only when the deadline looms, panic sets in and the adrenalin flows that the incentive is sufficient to get down to preparing the report and presentation.

Working at the last minute threatens the whole project. It assumes that all the data will be available in the way it is required. However, it is not unusual when putting pen to paper to find that there is some extra analysis required that could easily be obtained if only there was time. Working on the edge, there is no chance to re-run the analysis and it may never be carried out. A report written at the last minute is more likely to contain errors because there is no chance for someone else to read it or for sections to be rewritten if they are not up to scratch. Work that would otherwise be rejected goes through if a deadline is screaming.

For all these reasons, care must be taken to plan the timetable for the report and the presentation and to secure sufficient time for them to be carried out properly. This may mean working backwards from the date of the presentation and report delivery to ensure that a number of critical things happen. For example, a project will fall behind if the fieldwork is delayed, and the fieldwork cannot begin until a questionnaire has been designed and a sample frame worked out. Very often the critical path of a study is just two things: getting the questionnaire and sample frame prepared. Report writing and presentations are tasks in their own right but they should not be divorced from other parts of the research process. Working out a critical path at an early stage may be crucial for the preparation of a well written report and presentation.

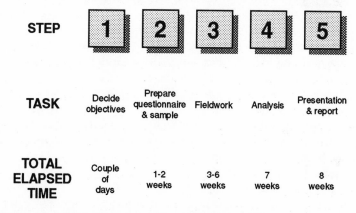

Figure 1.1 Critical steps in the research process

THE TIME REQUIRED TO PREPARE A REPORT AND PRESENTATION

There is no simple answer to the question of how long it takes to write a market research report. Very often report writing is not undertaken in one solid block. Time may be taken to answer phone calls or progress other projects that are in different stages of completion. The elapsed time from starting writing to finishing may be longer than the absolute time spent on the task.

A researcher with typing and wordprocessing skills will be able to prepare a report and presentation faster than someone who writes in longhand and is dependent on typists for the various edits. Getting to grips with the keyboard and wordprocessing is a must for every report writer.

Quantitative and qualitative market research reports take varying amounts of time. The time required to write up a quantitative study depends far more on the number of questions that need analysing one against the other and far less on whether there were 200 interviews or 1000. Tables are tables, whatever the size of the sample. Qualitative reports, however, require the researcher to plough through lengthy transcripts to pick up points hidden deep and scattered wide. Almost any competent report writer can pick up the analysis of a quantitative study and write a report but the best qualitative reports are written by the researcher who moderated the groups and carried out depth interviews. In general it is easier and quicker to write up a quantitative study than a qualitative one.

The skill and experience of the researcher are two other variables which affect the time required to write a report or prepare a presentation. Someone who is strong and experienced in report writing will be able to get through a report in half the time of someone who is new to the work.

When all the analysis has been carried out and it is just a question of putting the report together, it would be reasonable to expect a skilled researcher to be able to write between 1500 and 3000 words per day. Bearing these factors in mind, the table opposite gives some approximation of the time required to prepare three different types of reports.

The time required to prepare the presentation depends very much on whether the report (or at least the bones of it) has already been written. Working from a finished or nearly completed report, it should be possible to get a presentation of around 30 charts together in one to two days. Of course, presentations are put together much quicker than this by simply copying chunks of text straight out of a report. This is not the way to prepare a good presentation of market research work and it is usually caused by poor planning at the beginning, which means that there is insufficient time at the end.

TABLE 1.1 EXAMPLES OF TIME REQUIRED TO WRITE MARKET RESEARCH REPORTS

Type of report	Days to write report
Quantitative study with 30 questions (20 pages — 4–5000 words)	2–3
Qualitative study with four group discussions (20 pages — 6–8000 words)	2–4
International business-to-business project with desk research, interviews with producers, distributors and end users (80 pages — 15–20,000 words)	6–9

It has been assumed that:

1. The report writer is experienced and types directly into a computer.
2. The analysis has been completed prior to report writing.
3. The report is written in prose and not as bullet points.
4. The reports will include a mixture of text, tables and charts as appropriate.

Over the next six chapters of this book we deal with all aspects of report writing. Presentation skills and techniques are then covered in chapters 8 to 11.

REPORT WRITING

2

THE AUDIENCE AND ITS REQUIREMENTS

■

MIXED AUDIENCES AND DIFFERENT NEEDS

A report is for a reader, not for you. Reports have a specific audience. This can present problems because the audience could be mixed in composition, with very different needs. For example, a customer satisfaction survey commissioned by a large public company may be initiated by the board or the marketing director. The person with whom the researcher has most contact will not necessarily be the person who initiated the study, but someone who understands the market research process such as a market research manager, marketing services manager or marketing manager. He/she briefs the researcher, evaluates the proposals and steers the project as it is carried out. From the researcher's point of view, this could be the only point of contact and the final report may reflect what it is thought the market research manager wants. However, the principal audience is in the higher echelons. The board will have its own requirements from the study and the chances are they are much broader than those of the market research manager.

Understandably, the market research manager will want to ensure that the research is carried out thoroughly and that it covers all the issues. Getting down to detail will be important at this level. The higher up the organisation, the greater will be the interest in what the next steps should be and not the process of how the information was obtained or the nitty gritty of the findings. This means that a market research report can have many readers at different levels in an organisation and it needs to satisfy their many different requirements. Sometimes these different needs can be catered for by special sections of the report — an Executive Summary at the front for those who want a quick insight into the findings, conclusions and recommendations, and the body of findings and the appendices for those who need the detail for organising the plan of action.

WHAT AUDIENCES WANT FROM MARKET RESEARCH REPORTS

As part of the research for writing this book, we wrote to people who commissioned market research and asked them what they liked and disliked about market research reports. We analysed replies from 100 respondents, 33 whose main function was market research/market analysis and 67 who had wider management responsibilities or were directors. The results in the table below are issues mentioned by more than 15 per cent of each sample and show that recipients of market research reports, irrespective of their job title, want reports which:

■   answer the brief;
■   are well-structured/clear;
■   say what it all means, ie interpret the findings rather than just report them.

When we looked lower down the list of priorities we found that market research managers were more concerned with the detail, eg typos, poor grammar and inaccuracies, than were the other managers who were more concerned that the report be easy to read and simple. Also, several market research managers wanted detailed and thorough reports, whereas this was not mentioned by those in other management positions.

The two differing views below on what makes a good market research report illustrate the point made earlier, that different people want different things from a market research report. The first person wants detail, whereas the second wants clear, action-oriented recommendations.

TABLE 2.1 WHAT MAKES A GOOD MARKET RESEARCH REPORT?

	Total	Market research managers	Other management/ directors
	% mentioning	% mentioning	% mentioning
Answers the brief	33	45	27
Clarity/clear structure	29	18	35
Interpretation/conclusions	27	18	31
Recommendations/action points	21	33	15
Concise/to the point	21	21	21
Graphics/well-presented	19	24	17
Clear, concise executive summary	18	21	17
Total	*	*	*
Sample size	100	33	67

* People mentioned several factors, therefore does not add up to 100.

(Likes) Detailed methodology — sample size, breakdown, etc. Clearly presented data, tabulated as well as graphs. Executive summary for those who don't want to read all the detail but it must be 'meaty' enough. (Dislikes) Where you get bar charts but not actual numbers. Not enough background info or data so you can't do further analysis. Bland executive summaries.

Manager, Research & Planning

(Likes) Action orientation. Knows its audience. Clarity. Displays an awareness of initial objectives but is mature and flexible enough to highlight related issues. (Dislikes) Illogical. No good summary. Too much methodology. Displays ignorance of the subject and objective of the research.

Business Analyst

Although you may not be able to satisfy everyone, by finding out from the client what they want and expect in terms of a report you stand a far better chance of success.

WHAT AUDIENCES DON'T WANT FROM MARKET RESEARCH REPORTS

The dislikes and gripes of people who are on the receiving end of reports are in the main the opposite of their likes. So, the main dislikes are reports that do not answer the brief, are too long/too full of padding or waffle, have an unclear structure/poor signposting, have a naïve or no interpretation and do not come to firm conclusions.

Many people have very specific hates, which might not be any great problem to others, such as poor grammar/punctuation/spelling, spurious conclusions that cannot be supported by the data, too many verbatims, jargon, too many tables, reports which are structured around the questionnaire rather than the objectives, stating the obvious rather than providing commentary, and not understanding the client's business.

DIFFERENT TYPES OF REPORT

BULLET POINT REPORTS

Conventionally, market research reports communicate findings using a narrative, written in prose, and supported by tables and diagrams where appropriate. The length of these reports may vary, much depending on the complexity and size of the job. This is not to say that large jobs with many interviews and costing a great deal need to be commensurate in length but it is likely that the larger the project, the more information there will be to report. There is an inevitable tendency among researchers to want to deliver value for money and this may be translated in the final report as volume and output. Volume does not equal value and it may be that the attempt to be thorough creates a labyrinthine report that is hard to wade through.

Most people who commission market research are professionals who know what is entailed in the work. They are not kidded by lots of words, especially if a lot of it is padding. It is important that researchers rid their minds of the notion that the people who commission them calculate a price per word or cost per kilo of report. One marketing director was quoted as saying that 'some writers think quantity is how to impress the recipient but they're wrong'.

Not everyone wants a report with a narrative in elegant sentences. Such reports require greater concentration and take longer to read. Far quicker to get through are summary reports made up of bullet points and charts. These communicate more information, faster, but they inevitably lack the thoroughness of description and comment that can be achieved in prose. Bullet point reports are popular with senior management and therefore are widely used by management consultants. There is a strong trend in America towards reports that provide a summary position backed by a personal presentation, rather than lengthy tomes of text.

It would be dangerous to assume that there is room for only one type of report and that over time the bullet point report will eclipse that written in prose. Each has its place and sometimes it is no effort to produce both types on the same project. Hand-outs of the charts used for the presentation may create a perfectly adequate summary report while another, fuller report, is available for those who need the detail of a reference document.

PROGRESS OR INTERIM REPORTS

At various points during the project, it is important that the researcher feeds back progress reports. If there is a wide audience for a project, it would be normal for a progress report to be made to just one or two people — a research co-ordinator or a steering committee. In the main these will be verbal reports and are made over the phone or face-to-face. Occasionally, a summary of the progress report will be given in writing but is likely to be just two or three pages, stapled in the corner. There is a deliberate aim to play down the presentation of the progress report because it should not become a substitute for the real thing, with people arriving at premature conclusions before all the information is collected and analysed.

Whether the progress report is delivered verbally and/or as a note, it is likely to cover the following subjects:

■ A quick reminder of the aims of the study and how it is being carried out.

■ A statement of the number of interviews that have been achieved together with some view on whether or not they are going according to plan. For example, it may be relevant to review the strike rate (the number of people who need to be approached in order to obtain a successful interview) and the quality of the information that is forthcoming.

■ A feel for the type of information that is being obtained, accepting that in most surveys it is not possible (indeed it is dangerous) to arrive at conclusions before all the work is complete.

■ A statement of how much is left to do and when it will be done. Here it will also be necessary to re-confirm or renegotiate delivery dates for the presentation and the written report.

DRAFT REPORTS

If time permits it can be useful to send a draft copy of the final report to the client prior to its wider publication. This is particularly useful if the report is going to be sent out before any presentation. A draft report has two main purposes: to allow the client to read the recommendations and comment on their feasibility from the company's point of view and to correct any incorrect assumptions or statements made by the researcher about the client company. For example, the client's organisational structure may have changed since the project was first commissioned and consequently certain recommendations could be inappropriate or already in place. Draft reports should certainly not be an opportunity for the researcher to off-load his/her responsibility for checking the report thoroughly.

3

COPING WITH A MOUNTAIN OF DATA

■

THE SOURCES OF DATA FOR MARKET RESEARCH REPORTS

The whole *raison d'être* of market research is to provide information to aid decision-making and so reduce business risk. Of course, business decisions are made every day on hunches and opinions and there is nothing wrong with that. Small decisions, those which must be taken immediately, and which are self-evident, do not require the cost, time and trouble of a market research project. However, there are many uncertainties in business that can be minimised with good, solid information and here market research comes into its own. Given time, money and ingenuity, market research can guide most business decisions, though in some areas it has a better track record than in others. For example, market research cannot give a definitive view of the future but it can provide a good analysis of the past and provide views on possible trends and this may be as good a picture of the future that anyone can expect. It cannot predict next year's fashions with any accuracy, as fashions are created through conditioning, but market research can show what size clothes people buy, where and when they buy them and what motivates their purchase.

Market research comes into its own in answering how many, who, where and what. In other words it is a proven tool for counting and measuring what is going on in the marketplace. This is the quantitative side of the market research process and it frequently involves hundreds, sometimes thousands, of interviews. The findings of these interviews are entered on to computers and cross-analysed to produce tables of results, from which reports are written.

Market research also has a good track record in explaining how and why things happen and in the main it does this using qualitative methods. Qualitative research involves small numbers of interviews, nearly always carried out face-to-face and which may be one-to-one or in small discussion groups of 7 to 10 people. The emphasis in qualitative research is to get underneath the skin of the subject by pursuing lines of questioning that arise in the interview or discussion itself. These interviews and group discussions may take an hour or more and are normally captured on tape with the final report prepared from the transcripts.

One of the Cinderella methods of data collection used by market researchers is desk research. Desk research, also referred to as secondary research, is the collection and interpretation of data that has already been published — that which is produced by the Government, trade associations, directories, trade journals, the press and multi-client reports, which are sold to all and sundry. Desk research is less glamorous than survey work and is often ignored by market research agencies which organise their businesses around the collection of their own information. However, desk research is a useful tool to those who know how and where to use it. It is inexpensive and information can be obtained quickly from libraries, government offices and on-line database searches.

The three main sources of market research data are shown in Table 3.1 opposite.

PROBLEMS OF TOO MUCH DATA

Sometimes market research is used to examine narrow subjects such as the preferred colour of a pack, the price sensitivity of a

TABLE 3.1 SOURCES OF MARKET RESEARCH DATA

Research approach	What is involved?	Application
Desk research	Collecting information from published and non-survey sources	Building a picture of the market, building a sample for a survey
Quantitative methods	Surveys of hundreds or more people carried out by self-completion question-naire, telephone interviews or face-to-face interviews in the street, home and business	Measuring what is going on, segmenting the market
Qualitative methods	Small numbers of depth interviews or group discussions	Finding out what people think and what motivates them to do things

product or the acceptability of an advert. In such circumstances the data required to answer the question is also likely to be focused and the report writing task is that much simpler. However, researchers also help to provide answers to much broader marketing problems, such as how to enter a new market, how to revive flagging sales, how to build a new brand, how to launch a new product, how to beat the competition and how to win share. These are usually complex problems in which many issues need to be covered and, for example, may include the assessment of a market size, the shares of suppliers, the distribution routes, prices at different levels in the market, the buying behaviour and so on. In such broad-ranging studies all three market research approaches may be used so that information is fed in from desk research, qualitative research and large-scale surveys. With eclectic methods of data collection it does not take long before the researcher's file of information on the subject grows inches thick.

In one respect, the less information a manager has on a subject, the easier it is to make a decision since there is no confusion by the facts. Conversely, a wealth of data can produce a confusing picture as the important issues are hidden or data from various sources is conflicting. If the forest of information is dense, it can be difficult to see a way out. With greater knowledge of a subject there is a growing awareness of how much is not known, as one question begets another.

The two qualities that are most needed by market research report writers are clarity of thinking and expression. Indeed, the two go together. Clarity comes from the confidence to be able to cut through the forest of data and home in on the essential. Deciding what should and should not be included in a report is tough for the novice report writer who is tempted to err on the side of caution and is likely to include it 'just in case'.

REDUCING THE MOUNTAIN

The starting point for reducing the mountain of data is for the researcher to have an awareness of what is available and where to find it. This is especially important for the working papers that are collected during the project and it demands careful filing systems. Files which begin as a few pieces of paper soon grow in volume and need transferring to an archive box. Within the box, working papers should be classified and kept in separate files so that they can be retrieved easily.

The researcher must work out a classification for the individual files in the archive box on subjects such as client matters (correspondence, the brief and the proposal), original copies of the questionnaires in their various versions, sample lists, background data from published sources, completed interview notes, tapes and questionnaires (in a large survey there would be insufficient space for these in the working papers and they would be kept separately), and tabulations of results. Occasionally the researcher may work on a study where it is appropriate to classify the files according to key subject area such as market size data, trends, information on the competition, etc but in the main, this type of data is seldom separable at the time of collection. Data covering a broad range of subjects is hidden within interview notes and in various articles. The time to draw the different subjects together is at the data analysis stage, which is just before the report is written.

The archive box and all the files within it must be clearly labelled with the job title and job number so that the researcher (as well as anyone else in his or her absence) can find something if required to do so. Researchers usually work on more than one project at a time and there is a great temptation to have these spread around the desk and office with the excuse that this makes them easily accessible. It is an unacceptable way of working as it raises the danger of papers from one study being misfiled in another, resulting in wasted time as they are hunted high and low.

As a research project nears conclusion, the working papers grow exponentially. Quantitative studies propagate piles of cross-tabulations showing the results of questions analysed one against the other. These tabulations can easily get out of hand and need containing by being selective about the cross-analysis specification. Before the cross-analysis takes place there is much to be said for carrying out a simple count of the numbers of people answering each question (referred to as a 'hole count') and using this to guide the specification of the cross-analysis. Checking the hole count will show the likely sample sizes for each answer and allow many tables to be abandoned at the specification stage.

Towards the end of the data collection stage of the study, the researcher will draw up a structure for the report (see Chapter 4) and this will form a framework for reviewing the contents of the working papers. The researcher will then be able to see more clearly how the pieces of the jig-saw fit together. There will be some subjects on which there is a veritable mass of information and other areas which are relatively sparse. Once again the researcher will need the confidence to jettison some of the profuse data so that no single subject swamps the report.

As each file in the working papers is examined, the vital pieces of information should be moved to the front where they can be accessed readily. Inch thick tabulations of data should be looked through and key findings highlighted with marker pen. In a similar way, important points in the transcripts of depth interviews and group discussions should be marked.

Once the researcher is satisfied that all the possible data has been collected within the allotted timetable and that it has been sorted and prioritised, it is time to think about writing. From here on there will be much distilling of the data, bringing together pieces to build a picture while reducing the mountain. The writing process begins with a report structure, which is the subject of the next chapter.

4

WORKING OUT A REPORT STRUCTURE

■

THE IMPORTANCE OF STRUCTURE

The word *structure* underpins the whole market research process. It is the structure which is applied to data collection and analysis that makes market research a discipline and raises it above that of the 'anything-goes/it's only commonsense/let's give it to a student' school. Structure is especially important in the writing of market research reports as it provides a framework into which the data can be slotted. It is the route map which takes the reader from one subject to another and finally to a conclusion. For the purposes of this discussion on report writing, the word structure is interchangeable with the table of contents.

The creation of a structure for the report precedes any writing and follows the data collection and analysis. The researcher who is managing the project will almost certainly have been thinking about the structure of the report from the very beginning. Occasionally an outline of the chapters of the proposed report is agreed before the research begins but in the main, the report structure is prepared just prior to writing up the findings.

There are a number of stages in the market research process when the researcher feels daunted. One is when the euphoria of being asked to carry out a project has passed and the realisation sinks in that it will not be easy. The second pit in the stomach occurs when the researcher has to make sense of what has been collected. The problem is working out what to say and how to say it — in other words, organising a structure for the report. As with all long roads that must be travelled, the distance is nothing, it is only the first step that is difficult. The first step is the creation of the table of contents. The structure of the contents provides a plan which, once established, will reduce the intimidation.

A SUGGESTED STRUCTURE

There is no single, accepted structure for a report. Some researchers argue vehemently that a summary should always be at the beginning; others believe that there should be some context for the reader before they read the summary, so they prefer to see an introduction as the first chapter. There are no hard and fast rules and the researcher must develop a structure which feels comfortable. A typical structure would be:

■ Title page.
■ Table of contents.
■ Summary.
■ Introduction.
■ Findings.
■ Conclusions and recommendations.
■ Appendices.

These are the main chapter headings and within them are sub-sections covering detailed issues. Each section or chapter and sub-section is identified numerically and a standard practice is to use a 'legal' notation with two levels of numbers. For example, a report on the burglar alarm market in France could use the following main section and sub-section headings:

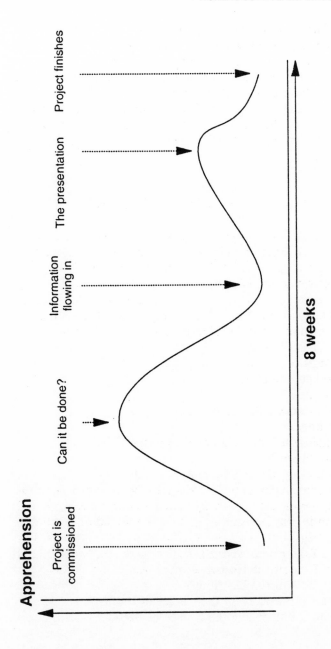

Figure 4.1 The Dromedary of Apprehension

THE MARKET FOR DOMESTIC BURGLAR ALARMS IN FRANCE

1   Summary

2   Introduction
2.1   Background
2.2   Objectives
2.3   Methods

3   Backcloth to the Market
3.1   Introduction
3.2   The Rise in Domestic Burglaries in France
3.3   Regional Variations in Domestic Burglaries
3.4   Types of Burglar Alarms Used in France

4   The Structure of the Market
4.1   Introduction
4.2   The Size of the Market
4.3   Segmentation of the Market
4.4   The Distribution of Burglar Alarms
4.5   Brands of Burglar Alarms Sold into the French
       Market

5   The Competitive Environment
5.1   Introduction
5.2   Profiles on Manufacturers Supplying the French
       Market
5.3   Profiles of Major Distributors of Alarms
5.4   Prices of Alarms

6   The Buying Decision
6.1   Introduction
6.2   The Role of the Alarm Installer
6.3   The Role of the Householder
6.4   The Role of the Distributor
6.5   Other Influencers on the Choice of Brand
6.6   Factors Influencing the Choice of Brand

We now describe the main structural headings that are used in a report.

THE TITLE PAGE

The title page may also be the front cover of the report. It is the first thing that people see and is, therefore, the shop window of the report. It needs to create an image of professionalism and engage the interest of the reader, encouraging people to pick it up and read. The title page must state clearly what the report is about and is best if short, to the point and slightly intriguing or tantalising. If the report is confidential, this should be stated clearly. The report may have a filing notation or job number, which could be tucked away in some corner of the title page.

Other information sometimes displayed on a title page is the person or company who has carried out the work and the name of the research sponsor. Finally, the date of issue should be shown.

TABLE OF CONTENTS

The table of contents of a report is a map describing the report structure. It is a listing of all main and sub-headings together with their page numbers. In a report with a large number of tables it is probably also appropriate to provide a listing. The table of contents should also mention any appendices.

SUMMARY

Reports of ten pages or more should have a summary containing all the salient points from the body of the document including the introduction, findings and conclusions. The summary is possibly the most important section of the report, taking pride of place at the front where it will be read by everyone. Indeed, some will read this section only. Although it is positioned at the front of the report, the summary is the last section to be written. Given its importance great care must be taken. It is most definitely not a section to be thrown together at the last minute when the researcher is tired of the project and ready to move on. It is worthwhile pausing at the end of writing the findings and before working on the summary, to recharge the batteries and take a fresh look at the whole picture.

The style and layout of the summary require careful attention. Summaries are generally in words but, depending on the objectives and findings, tables, charts or diagrams can be effective in adding impact. The summary can probably be broken down into 20 or so key points with as many paragraphs, each containing just a few sentences. Even though it is a summary, sentences should not be abbreviated.

The length of the summary will be in approximate proportion to that of the report. A 20-page report should aim for a single page summary while a 100-page report may require five pages. Of course, summaries can be shortened to half a page irrespective of the report length but brevity should not be at the expense of sense.

INTRODUCTION

Following on from the summary is a chapter that introduces the report telling the reader why the research was carried out, what the researcher set out to do and how the results have been achieved. These topics can be covered under three sub-sections; background, objectives and methods.

Within the 'background' sub-section the scene is set, describing the lead-up to the commissioning of the study. This may include a short account of the problem that was faced by the research sponsor, for example:

> Jones & Co are considering entering the French market for domestic burglar alarms. An investment of £1 million would be required in production and marketing resources. In order to evaluate the viability of the project Jones & Co require a full understanding of the French market for burglar alarms. Ace Research was commissioned to study the market against objectives agreed in a proposal dated January 1994.

The 'objectives' sub-section provides a statement of the overall aim of the study and the areas of information to be covered. It can be helpful for the reader to see a short statement of the aims expressed in just one or two sentences, such as:

> The broad objectives of the study were agreed in advance to be:
>
> To analyse the market for domestic burglar alarms in France, to indicate the opportunities for Jones & Co, the barriers which could prevent these opportunities being realised and to make recommendations on if and how the Company could enter the market.

There may then be a listing of some of the sub-objectives that had to be achieved if the overall aim was to be fulfilled. For example:

■   To assess market size and segmentation over the last three years.

■   To assess market shares and provide a profile of the competing suppliers.

■   To predict future trends over the next three years.

■   To show the importance of installers, builders and householders in the decision-making process which results in the selection of a certain make of alarm.

■   To show what motivates the specifiers of domestic burglar alarms in their choice of a certain make/supplier.

■   To recommend a suitable product range for Jones & Co.

■   To recommend sales targets for each of the next three years and show the marketing strategies that will enable these to be achieved.

The 'methods' sub-section of the Introduction would describe the methods by which the information was obtained, highlighting any deviations from the approach given in the original proposal. Some of the sources that could be summarised in the section on methods are:

■   **Secondary research.** The range of desk research sources should be mentioned but not over specified as it is better to include a detailed bibliography in an appendix.

■   **Primary research.** Here it would be appropriate to summarise the qualitative and quantitative research methods that were used including the number of telephone, face-to-face interviews, self-completion questionnaires or group discussions. A copy of the questionnaire is useful to a reader and should be available in an appendix.

Depending on the subject or type of report, the length of the method section can vary enormously. In some industrial projects the method may merely involve desk research and a small number of informal interviews. In consumer studies it is customary to include details of the sample profile, how and when the data were collected, whether the data is weighted, and whether respondents were given any incentives. It may also be appropriate in some cases to include other information about the sample or method, which might be useful information in itself. For example, if a particular type of respondent was particularly difficult to find, this could indicate the problems the company may face in selling its products.

However, a word of caution. A weakness of market researchers is a method orientation which, unless curbed, could turn into a two to three page, blow-by-blow account of how the research was carried out. In the main, a half to a full page of text will be more than sufficient.

FINDINGS

The findings constitute the body of the report. They present all the relevant facts and opinions collected by the researcher but make no attempt to show the implications for the research sponsor's plans since this is the role of the conclusions.

The subjects under discussion in the findings will, of course, vary from project to project. Sometimes they cover market size, market share and market trends; at other times they may be confined to image or attitudinal data. Whatever the content, the sequence should be logical. For example, buyers' awareness of companies should be discussed before any consideration of attitudes to the companies. The results of open-ended questioning should precede those from prompted questions. All the time the findings will take the reader from the general to the particular.

The findings attempt to bring to the fore any patterns in the industry or in the responses. This inevitably means that some generalisations will be made, although this does not preclude specific comments to exemplify and highlight points. Quotes (also known as verbatim comments or just verbatims) add authenticity to a report and make the results all the more credible. To make sense of the quotes it may be necessary to attribute them to a certain type of person or company but it is important that respondents' anonymity is preserved. Thus, it is acceptable to say: 'Richardson's pumps are rubbish because they are always breaking down.' (Plant Engineer, Power Station), and not acceptable to say: 'Richardson's pumps are rubbish because they are always breaking down.' (John Smith, Plant Engineer, Fawley Power Station). Quoted comments are especially useful for enlivening and adding personality to a report. They forcibly remind the reader that the views being expressed are those of respondents and not the researcher. The onus is on the researcher to ensure that the quotes genuinely reflect the general view and have not been selected to support a personal prejudice. It is also important to remember that a whole string of quotes should not be used without providing a meaningful commentary.

CONCLUSIONS AND RECOMMENDATIONS

Conclusions are the showcase of a research report. They provide an opportunity for the researcher to sparkle over and beyond some of the more pedestrian information, which very often forms the body of the findings. The Conclusions section of a market research report may be relatively short but it is likely to be well read and scrutinised. After all, it is in the Conclusions that the meaning of the report is brought out and the way forward is suggested.

The Conclusions draw together the findings. They are not simply a summary, although they may be arrived at by leading with a summary of the findings. Rather they provide the opportunity to relate the subject of interest to the findings and move beyond these to offer recommendations with suggested solutions to specific problems. Conclusions are, therefore, evaluative, using facts but also containing value judgements and it is very important that these are clearly separated from the findings.

The market researcher is involved in the preparation of two types of research project, both needing different approaches within the Conclusions.

■ **Research to improve a client's knowledge of a market.**
Often the researcher is not asked to solve a business
problem; all that is required is a detailed briefing on the
facts of the market, which will help the research sponsor
to make a decision now or in the future. In such a report,
the Conclusions, though drawing heavily on the findings,
should not be a mere summary. Certainly, some summary
will be made in the Conclusions as the researcher re-states
the main issues and trends. However, there should also be
an attempt to select elements of particular importance to
the Client's business, and even to show the marketing
implications. In this way the researcher interprets and
possibly shows options, but stops short of suggesting
what the client's next moves should be.

■ **Research to solve a specific research problem.** Conventional problem solving in business follows a number of
steps. The facts on the company and the market lead to a
consideration of the options, an option is selected and an
action plan follows. The facts are, of course, highly
relevant to arriving at the optimum decision but the
actual plan may have to fit in with what is politically
expedient within the client company.

Researchers, especially those working at arm's length to the
client company, may not have access to all the company's
limitations, resources and objectives. The researcher should, in
this case, concentrate on the facts about the market. To this
extent the conclusions are more objective and avoid the political
problems of in-company wrangling. Rather than turn up on the
day of the presentation with a report, a pile of acetates and a
host of recommendations, these should first be checked out for
logic and feasibility with the client. This way some thunder may
be lost, but 'so what' if the recommendations are more likely to
be accepted.

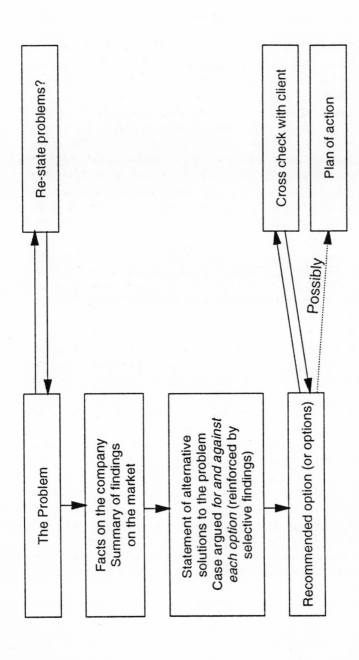

Figure 4.2 Steps in arriving at conclusions for a market research report

APPENDICES

Appendices are used to contain data which, while of possible value or interest to the reader, is not essential to the presentation of the findings or conclusions. They could include:

- **Questionnaires.** Readers frequently find it helpful to be able to refer to how questions were asked.
- **Sources of information.** These provide the study with credibility and may be useful to a future researcher who has to follow up the work. They may be divided into sections such as bibliography and details of the sample. In industrial work a list of respondent companies is often included, although not the name of the respondents themselves.
- **Statistical methods.** These are notes on how data has been calculated, for example significance tests or methods of weighting the data. If the report contains a statistical forecast, the detailed working may be described in the appendix.
- **Detailed tables.** Lengthy statistical tables may be better in the appendix although key data should be in the findings.
- **Financial profiles.** As with the statistical data, financial profiles on companies should be provided in the appendix.
- **Descriptions and definitions.** Lengthy descriptions of processes should be in the appendix.
- **Product literature.** Sometimes it is relevant to include product literature in a report.

Appendices should not exist in isolation. They should be referred to in the text and only be included if they truly supplement the findings. There are no hard and fast rules for the length of appendices but they are not a dumping ground for vaguely related material and a reasonable balance should be maintained between the length of the report and that of the appendix.

THE LOGIC OF PREPARING A REPORT

A good report is a planned report. The more detailed the planning, the better will be the finished document and the easier it will be to write and read. A mistake that many researchers make in attacking the findings is to write up the results in the sequence that the research was carried out — desk research in one section, qualitative research in another, and quantitative in yet another. The quantitative research may similarly follow the format of the questionnaire, each question forming a small section as the researcher ploughs through it in chronological order. The result would be:

TABLE 4.1 THE EASY (BUT NOT THE BEST) WAY TO STRUCTURE FINDINGS

A	B	C
Desk research	Qualitative findings	Quantitative findings

This type of structure would contain everything that was discovered in the study but would be repetitive for the reader. Some of the subjects covered in the desk research may well be mentioned later in the qualitative research. So too the same issues raised within the qualitative research section would crop up yet again in the quantitative section, this time wrapped up in numbers. It is far better to bring together the findings from the different sources to build a picture within chapter headings that have meaning to the reader. For example, desk research may be the principal source of data used in the chapter on market size and market structure. The chapter on buying behaviour may draw on findings from both the qualitative and quantitative parts of the study, with no input from desk research. However, the chapter on trends would draw on all sources: desk research, qualitative and quantitative.

TABLE 4.2 THE MORE DIFFICULT (BUT BEST) WAY TO STRUCTURE FINDINGS

Chapter 1	Chapter 2	Chapter 3	Chapter 4
Market size	Market organisation	Buying behaviour	Trends
A	A	B + C	A + B + C

The main chapter headings and sub-headings for a report will come out of the knowledge that has been built up on the subject, but reference should also be made to the initial proposal. Bearing all these things in mind, the researcher should begin to construct the report's main headings and the sub-headings. At this early stage, when the map of the report is being formed, it is useful to write a word or two summarising the subjects to be covered in each sub-section. The structure as it stands before any words have been written is only a starter and it is probable that changes will be made, with new sub-sections added and others deleted, as the very act of writing throws up new and better ways of presenting the data.

At this stage it is worthwhile pausing and considering the purpose of the headings and sub-headings. These titles are there to help the reader quickly find a way through the report. They should be short and snappy, wherever possible just half a dozen words or so and limited to just one line. The precise wording of the headings is very much up to the author. Some like to draw the reader forward with enticing titles such as *What Are The Chances Of Premium Prices?* while others prefer their titles to be more descriptive, for example *Opportunities For Premium Prices*.

Once the bones of the structure are laid out with headings and sub-headings, notes can be compiled on the information to be contained in each section. As a guide, a reader should not have to face a page full of dense text; at least one sub-heading should break a page with a headline. If the narrative in a sub-section exceeds 300 words, the author should think of splitting it and creating a new one.

5

TEXT, TABLES AND GRAPHICS

■

Reports contain text, often supported by tables and charts or diagrams. Careful attention to the presentation of the data will impress the reader and help the findings achieve greater conviction.

There is no such thing as the correct balance between text, tables and graphics. The use of each depends on three main factors:

■ The type of research/subject matter.
■ The type of data.
■ The wishes and expectations of the client.

TYPE OF RESEARCH

In a *qualitative* report it is customary to write a narrative report interspersed with verbatim quotes to illustrate the points being made and the only decision the writer has to make is how many chapter or sections there should be and which topics will be dealt with under each. However, qualitative reports can also be enhanced by diagrams which communicate more readily and powerfully a complex issue such as the buying decision for a house (see Figure 9.1 in Chapter 9).

With a *quantitative* report a decision has to be made as to whether to use tables or diagrams or both and whether they will be included in the text, appear only in the appendices and be cross-referenced or will appear on a facing page. The most common practice is to combine tables and text, although graphics are often placed on a facing page.

THE TYPE OF DATA

The purpose of diagrams is to give a quick visual impression as to a pattern or a trend in data. They can simplify and more quickly communicate figures than can words or tables. However, they are not always the answer and there may be occasions when a table is more acceptable. Take for example the balance sheet or profit and loss account of a company. We expect to see this laid out as a table in a conventional format: a diagram could not possibly show all the detail required. As a rule anything required for reference (where the reader needs precise figures rather than a broad idea) is better left as a table. So, a list of prices or currency conversion rates are more suited to a conventional tabular format.

CLIENT WISHES

The importance of knowing what your client wants and expects in terms of his or her report cannot be stressed too much. The culture of the client organisation may dictate the preferred type of report. For example, some organisations want mostly graphics and little text, some are keen on detailed tables and feel that graphics 'fudge' the facts and others like a good narrative report with the minimum of tables or diagrams. As we have already seen in Chapter 2, some clients complain that reports are too long and wordy, whereas others want all the detail.

HOW TO LAY OUT AN EFFECTIVE TABLE

If the report is heavily statistical, the tables should be prepared first and assembled into the order they will appear in the report. The report is now hung around the tables.

Tables provide a shorthand means of communicating figures. They should be used to show patterns and exceptions. The researcher should use tables wherever possible, bearing in mind a number of rules:

- **Keep it simple.** Two or three simple tables are better than one that is complicated.
- **Label all tables.** Tables should have headings clearly stating what they show. The headings should also show the date of the data if relevant, for example, attributing a table showing the market size to the year to which it refers. Columns within the tables should have headings showing whether they are tonnes, numbers, monetary values, etc. Some researchers like to see the size of the sample at the head of the columns so that the reader is immediately allowed to judge the robustness of the data while others prefer to keep the sample information at the bottom of the table so that it does not interfere with the percentages. Sources of information should be shown below the tables.
- **Show totals.** A reader's eye will move up and down a column. Columns of data should all have a total to show that they add to 100 per cent or, in the case of questions where people can give more than one response (multi-response), an asterisk or some notation to indicate why it exceeds 100 per cent.
- **Use rounded figures.** In the main, quantitative data in market research reports provides comparative information which allows the reader to see how groups of people act or think. The data is not always statistically significant, especially if the sample is broken into sub-groups of age, social class, or, in business-to-business markets, users from different industries. It would be a

pretence of accuracy to present this data to decimal places and in any case, to do so would make it harder for the eye to pick out the general patterns of response. Through rounding off the figures, some columns may not add to 100 per cent and the researcher needs a policy on whether to reassign the under or over percentage points to make everything add to 100 per cent. If the figures are to be made to add to 100, the adjustment should be on the highest figures in the column since these will be less influenced by the adjustment.

■ **Order rows and columns by size.** A table with data in decreasing order of importance is easier to absorb than one presented in random fashion. Again, the aim is to illustrate a pattern. Ordered rows do this much more effectively than randomly distributed rows. Of course, there are exceptions to ordering data by size of response. Data would not be ordered if the table presented the results of an attitude scale ranging from Very Good, Quite Good through to Quite Poor and Very Poor. The sequence of the scale would always remain the same whatever the result.

■ **Draw lines to separate data.** A large table with a number of vertical columns may be made easier to read if the columns are distinguished by lines.

Figure 5.1 is an example of a badly constructed table. Figure 5.2 shows the same data in a more user-friendly format.

HOW TO DECIDE WHICH TYPE OF DIAGRAM TO USE

Assuming that the writer has decided to use diagrams in the report (or a mixture of diagrams and tables), the decision then needs to be taken as to which type of diagram or chart is the most appropriate for the data being communicated. The choice between the different types of chart is not always clear-cut. We now look at the main types of charts and the uses to which they are commonly put.

Dissatisfaction with motor, personal accident or sickness and holiday insurance

	motor	pers. acc./ sick	holiday
unweighted bases; those dissatisfied	149	28	33
cause of dissatisfaction	%	%	%
misled by broker/salesman into taking unnecessary/expensive policy	1.2	16.3	
special conditions imposed (inc. excess)	6.45	7.0	6.6
cost of policy/premium increase	39.3	27.4	11.4
claim not covered by policy	1.6	9.9	15.2
claim not met in full	6.7	17.4	17.1
long delay in dealing with claim	19.8	19.1	29.0
other complaints	26.9	12.6	10.2
not stated	6.1	10.8	24.4

Figure 5.1 Badly constructed table

Reasons For Dissatisfaction With Insurance Policies

Cause of dissatisfaction	Type of policy		
	Motor	Accident/ sickness	Holiday
	%	%	%
Cost of policy/premium increase	39	27	11
Delay in dealing with claim	20	19	29
Claim not met in full	7	17	17
Claim not covered by policy	2	10	15
Special conditions imposed	6	7	7
Misled into expensive policy	1	16	-
Other complaints	27	13	10
Not stated	6	11	24
Total	*	*	*
Sample size	149	28	33

*Multi-response and therefore exceeds 100 per cent
Source: *The Insurance Handbook.*

Figure 5.2 Revised table

GRAPHS

Graphs are used to show trends in figures over a period of time, eg changes in population, sales of motor vehicles, a country's GDP, etc. Although they perform the same function as bar charts they are usually used when there are a larger number of data points.

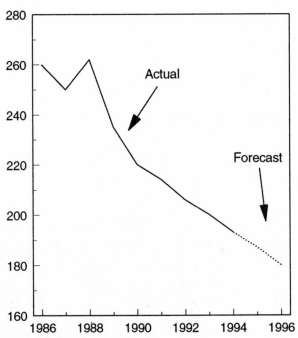

Source: Business & Market Research plc
Figure 5.3 Trends in the UK market

For example, sales plotted over a 20 year period can be comfortably accommodated on a graph, whereas 20 bars would be very cluttered and it would be harder for the reader to pick out trends. With a graph the eye can pick out the trend and project it forward, so obtaining a feel for the future. However, graphs lose all their clarity and simplicity if too many lines are put on them, particularly when they are in black and white and the different trend lines are shown by a variety of dots and dashes, or when the lines are close together and cross. A maximum of three or four lines is to be recommended.

PIE CHARTS

These are used when there is a requirement to show parts of a whole, ie the data must add up to 100 per cent. Their most popular use is for market shares of particular brands/suppliers or to show sales in a market segment between different sectors. In many industrial markets researchers cannot estimate market shares to closer than 5 or 10 per cent and here the pie diagram

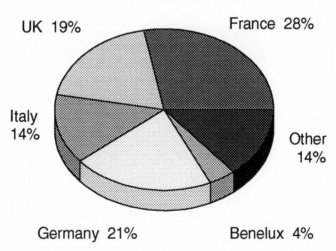

Source: *Euromonitor*
Figure 5.4 The European market for liquid detergents

converts the spurious precision of a table into a spatial
delineation of the differences between the companies, which is
usually more important than the actual share percentages *per se*.

BAR CHARTS

Bar charts are very versatile and there are several different
types, eg horizontal, vertical, divided, double, etc. In vertical
form a simple bar chart might have just one bar which is divided
up to show its component parts, rather like a pie chart.

Responses to a particular question are often shown by
horizontal bars, eg mean scores representing the importance of
factors in the buying decision. Two bars can be grouped

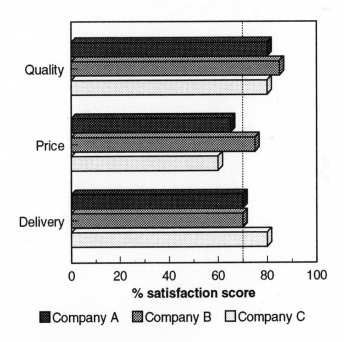

Source: Business & Market Research plc
Figure 5.5 Rating of companies

together to show the same responses but comparing this year with previous years or the performances of two suppliers.

Horizontal bar charts are also a very useful way of presenting customer satisfaction data. The factors most important to customers can be listed in descending order of importance and the supplier's scores on these factors shown falling either side of a line denoting a satisfactory performance.

Bar charts have an important advantage over line graphs in that they can show a trend and movements within segments.

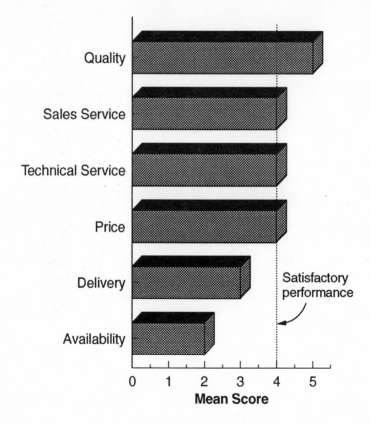

Figure 5.6 Factors influencing the buying decision

Market size
(tonnes)

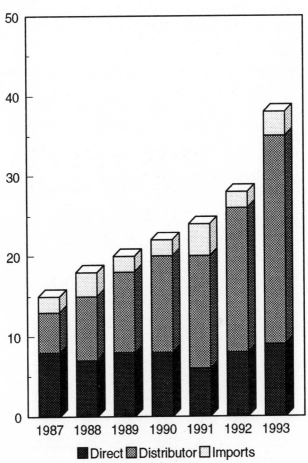

Source: Business & Market Research plc
Figure 5.7 Market and distribution trends

Splitting up each column shows the trend, while lining up the vertical bars next to each other will show how both the whole and the component parts of a market have moved over time.

CHARTS COMPARING TWO VARIABLES

In marketing we often need to position companies or see the relationship between two variables. For this we need a diagram with the usual x and y axes but this time we locate points on the graph where the two points meet. In this way it possible to show, for example, the positioning of companies on the two key factors of price and quality.

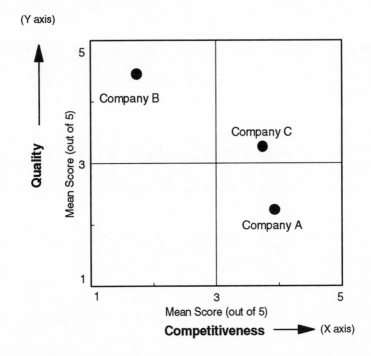

Source: Business & Market Research plc

Figure 5.8 The positioning of three companies

ORGANISATIONAL CHARTS

These show the flow of data. They could show the stages in a project, the management organisation of a company or the structure of a market.

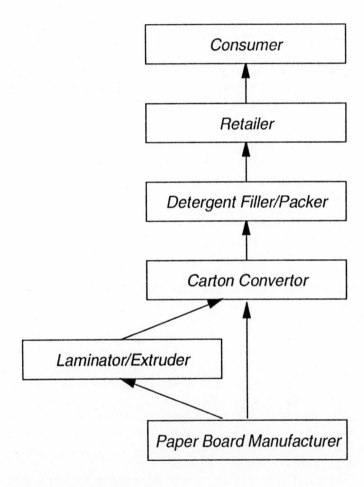

Figure 5.9 The supply chain

THREE TIPS ON PRODUCING GOOD DIAGRAMS

- **Give the diagram a clear title.** Charts, as tables, need a title which says simply and clearly what is being portrayed. This is especially important when the diagram is on a facing page rather than integrated into the text.
- **Clearly mark the scale.** Scales should be marked and there must be a key or words on the chart to tell the reader what is what. Wherever possible keep the words horizontal.
- **Keep them simple.** Diagrams will not work if they contain too much information, have too many lines or too many different types of shading. With presentation charts in colour it is easier to get away with more detail, but if the report is to be produced in black and white then care needs to be taken in the choice of shading, so that bars or slices of the pie can be distinguished easily.

Do not be afraid to split up the data in one table to make several diagrams, they will undoubtedly be much clearer and simpler, which are the key rules for producing good diagrams.

WHERE TO POSITION TEXT IN CONJUNCTION WITH TABLES AND GRAPHICS

A table or diagram should be preceded by explanatory narrative so that the reader gains a quick understanding of the importance of what is being conveyed. Preceding tables by text does not follow the natural sequence of working, which is to prepare the table and then write about it. However, it is irritating to readers, if they are faced with a table and work out its meaning, to find out that their efforts were wasted because an explanation exists below it.

When commenting on tabulations or writing about group discussions, it is usual to comment on what most people said and then move on to specific comments. For example, consider the table below and then look at commentaries A and B.

TABLE 5.1 NUMBER OF VEHICLES BOUGHT PER WEEK

Number of vehicles	Total %	North %	Midlands %	South %
1–2	55	65	55	65
3–4	40	30	45	35
5	5	5	0	0
Over 6	0	0	0	0
Total	*100*	*100*	*100*	*100*

Sample size: 150 dealers

A. Only 5 per cent of our sample purchased 5 vehicles per week and they were all based in the North. Nobody purchased more than 5 vehicles and most purchased between 1 and 4.

B. Nearly all (95 per cent) dealers bought between 1 and 4 vehicles a week and there was little difference in buying habits between regions. None of them purchased more than 5 vehicles.

There are no prizes for observing that commentary B is a better interpretation of the data. Having said this, all rules are there to be broken and there may be instances when the minority view is most relevant and worthy of comment.

Many clients bemoan the fact that they have a report full of facts and tables but are left wondering what it all means. Often the client (particularly one inexperienced in using research) needs guidance as to what importance to attribute to certain findings. For example, if suppliers are being scored on a 1–5 scale on various aspects of their performance, what does a mean score of 3.2 signify? Previous experience of other surveys could indicate that market leaders can be expected to score over 4. Adding this note of guidance helps the reader to make greater sense of the data.

It also helps the reader if the answers from one question are cross-referenced to others where appropriate. For example, if the results from an open-ended question on why a particular product was chosen are at variance with a prompted question on the same subject, some explanation should be given to help the reader make sense of the data.

TIPS ON THE USE OF ATTENTION GRABBERS

Sometimes photographs, illustrations and diagrams have to be included in reports in order for them to make any sense. For example, it is difficult for the reader to grasp the merits of Pack A rather than Pack B, if there is no visual record in the report. The advent of widespread colour photocopying has made this process much quicker.

However, photographs and other illustrative material can be used to liven up and improve the impact of many types of research and not just pack testing and advertising research. For example, a photograph of the antiquated machinery still being used in a factory in Romania could bring home to a potential British exporter the problems they will encounter in trying to sell their sophisticated tools into that market, much more than mere words.

We ought also to sound a word of warning. Too many photographs and other illustrations, which do not add anything to the written word, can be counter-productive and regarded as 'gimmicky'.

6

GETTING THE REPORT TO READ WELL

■

Some people are born with the ability to write well while others struggle. By the time you enter into market research your basic writing style will be developed. It will be different to other people's. Teaching sentence construction and basic grammar is far beyond the scope of a short book like this. However, whether you feel writing comes easily to you or whether every sentence is a trial, we can give you some tips that will make a substantial difference to the readability of your market research reports.

THE DIFFERENCES BETWEEN REPORT WRITING AND NOVELS

The overall aim of any business report is to communicate facts or opinions clearly and simply to another person or persons in the shortest possible time. The big difference between report writing and novels is the time element. A good novel often takes some 'getting into' and a thriller can keep the reader guessing until the last page. Nobody cares about the length of the novel as long as it is interesting or entertaining. Write a market research report in the same way and your future as a market researcher is doomed!

There are many acclaimed classic novels that most people would have great difficulty in understanding. They contain words that the average person has never seen before. The meaning of the book might be lost on many. Many of us have a secret desire to write a novel but whatever you do, do not try to display this budding talent in your reports. If your readers do not understand certain words in the document, it does not demonstrate that you are clever, rather that you have no sympathy for them. And if they are fee-paying clients or your bosses, they may not appreciate your lack of concern. If the meaning is not crystal clear from the outset then you have failed, and it is not your reader who is lacking in intelligence.

THE IMPORTANCE OF WRITING GOOD PROSE

As we have already seen, the objective of a report is to communicate information and opinion clearly and quickly. A good report structure and layout should ensure that the reader is following a logical train of thought. However, all this can be wasted if the actual English is poor and the reader has to re-read sentences in order to understand them. The purpose of writing good prose is to ensure there is no ambiguity and, therefore, make the reader's task easier.

In his book on business writing[1] The American writer Martyn Stuckey gives a good, if slightly exaggerated, example of the train of events that could be set in motion by an ambiguous memo circulated widely within a company. He makes the valid point of asking whose time is more valuable, the report writer's or the reader's? If you pass on a sloppy report to a senior colleague, or worse still a client, you are sending the message that they have the time, but you do not, to unravel your rambling, complex sentences or check your spelling errors.

---

[1] Stuckey, Martyn (1992) *The Basics of Business Writing*, Amacom, New York.

There are two main things you can do to improve your prose:

■   Avoid complicated words, jargon and slang.
■   Keep the sentences short.

There are no gold stars for using the longest, most obscure words in the dictionary. Where there is a short word it should be used. Jargon should not be used, unless it really cannot be avoided. Likewise, slang is usually inappropriate, except in verbatim comments.

Again as a general rule, sentences should be short rather than long. If you have difficulty in keeping sentences to a manageable length, bullet points are a useful device. They have the advantages of:

■   Letting the reader see immediately how many points you are making.
■   Relieving the boredom of long pages of dense text.
■   Making each point simple and easy to understand.

As with all devices, used too much they can make the report stilted. However, in the commercial world, most clients would rather read a snappy report than a literary work with long, convoluted sentences.

The Complete Plain Words by Sir Ernest Gowers (Pelican Books, 1977) is a useful book on report writing of any kind, not just market research.

COMMON MISTAKES OF STYLE AND GRAMMAR

There are four very common errors of grammar and style (we deal with punctuation separately in the next section) which we come across frequently in our editing of reports. Some of them are quite trivial and are simply irritating. However, others can hinder understanding of what the writer is trying to communicate. Ranked in order of their importance to good report writing, they are:

■   Poor sentence construction.
■   Ambiguous sentences.
■   Cliches — meaningless phrases.
■   How to refer to a company.

POOR SENTENCE CONSTRUCTION

As a general rule sentences should be constructed in the following way: subject, verb, object. This of course makes them active rather than passive. At one time it was the norm to write reports in the passive tense, eg '50 respondents were interviewed by our telephone researchers' rather than in the active 'our telephone researchers interviewed 50 respondents'. In our view it is much clearer to use the active form. Sometimes the use of the passive results in very clumsy English: 'Respondents were asked as to their purchases of tyres on a monthly basis.' Better wording would have been: 'We asked respondents how many tyres they bought each month.'

All sentences must have a verb. Although this may seem blindingly obvious, we frequently come across sentences with none, as in the following example: 'There have been many acquisitions and mergers over the last few years, such as the one currently in the headlines. Similarly the absorption of Firelite by Notifier.'

AMBIGUOUS SENTENCES

There are instances when the reader is left wondering what the 'this' refers to or who the 'they' are. Consider the ambiguities in the following example:

There were three different ways of customers giving instructions to the bank:

■   half gave instructions in person
■   fax is little used
■   the rest use phone and fax

This has implications if the bank wants to change the way the accounts are run.

The 'this' is rather ambiguous. Is it trying to say that the high level of personal contact has implications for the bank or the low usage of fax? Also, saying that fax is little used and then saying that the rest use phone and fax is somewhat confusing for the reader. This is a case where more words need to be used to ensure that there is no misunderstanding. It would have been better to write:

There were three different ways customers gave instructions to the bank:

■ half gave instructions in person
■ most of the rest used a combination of phone and fax
■ fax was seldom the only method used

The current high level of personal contact has implications for the bank if it wants to change the way the accounts are handled.

CLICHES AND MEANINGLESS PHRASES

We all hate them but we use them nonetheless. They come into the class of irritations rather than serious faults. However, if used extensively the sentences in a report can become so long and cliche-ridden that the true meaning of the sentence gets lost.

Do you prefer to read: 'In essence, at this moment in time, the position with regard to the factory is being given serious consideration by the management' or, 'the management are considering what to do with the factory'?

We do not intend to provide a comprehensive glossary of phrases not to use (there is a very comprehensive one in Martyn Stuckey's book referred to earlier) but when you are writing and editing reports always try to use the simplest and/or shortest word or phrase.

HOW TO REFER TO A COMPANY

A company is singular and neuter: it should be referred to as 'it' and not 'they', although it is common practice to talk about 'they'. You should talk about 'Smith Ltd and its plans' and not 'their plans'. This is a difficult habit to kick if you have spent your whole life referring to a company as a plural entity. If you cannot change it does not really matter which convention is adopted, as long as it is consistent throughout the report.

Another related problem some people have is knowing when to use 'who' and when to use 'which'. 'Who' is always used when referring to people, eg the people who go to work in the city and 'which' to things, eg the company which employs 100 people.

THE IMPORTANCE OF CORRECT PUNCTUATION

One common reason why reports are unclear is poor punctuation. The main role of punctuation is: '... to make perfectly clear the construction of the written words. If this function is properly fulfilled, then automatically all risk of ambiguity will be avoided and the appropriate pauses will be indicated to the reader, when they are not so optional as to be left to him to supply.'[2]

As others have written whole books on the subject, we will confine ourselves to looking at the most common errors that confront the report editor and the reader most frequently. We apologise to those who think we are insulting their intelligence but many market researchers commit the most basic punctuation errors in these five areas:

■ commas
■ capitals
■ hyphens

---

[2] Carey, GV (1976) *Mind The Stop*, Penguin, London.

■ colons and semi-colons
■ apostrophes.

COMMAS

A common mistake is to separate by a comma two clauses that are not linked by a conjunction, as in the following example: 'The man entered the house, he was very cold.' There are three correct ways you could write this sentence, depending on personal preference and your style. You can either put a full-stop or semi-colon between the clauses or put in the word 'and'.

You should separate subordinate clauses from the main clause by commas at both ends. In many reports commas appear indiscriminately at one end or another. A good way of looking at this is to ask yourself whether taking out the words between the commas would still leave the sentence making sense. The following sentence illustrates the correct usage: 'Meanwhile, unless the Government takes firm action, the situation will steadily deteriorate.'

The main rule with commas is to re-read your sentence for sense. Have the commas you have put in (or left out) altered the intended meaning? The use of commas in the following sentences illustrates how meaning can be subtly altered: 'However the incident may be explained, the impression it has left is unfortunate. However, the incident may be explained in such a way as to satisfy public opinion.'

CAPITALS

Capital letters should be used for proper names, eg names of people, names of places, brand names, etc. Beyond this, their use becomes more tricky and there are no hard and fast rules. The best advice we can give is, again, to be consistent.

One useful pointer is whether the use is general or specific. For example, if you say: 'Paul Hague, Chairman of Business & Market Research' then the job title should be in capitals as it is specific. However, if you just want to refer to that job function in general, a small letter is usually best: The problem with being a chairman is that ...'. Government is another potential pitfall. With a capital G it usually means the people in power, eg: 'The Government has recently brought in a new regulation on ...' If, on the other hand, you want to talk in general terms about 'the role of government in the democratic world', you would not use a capital letter.

HYPHENS

You use hyphens when you want to tell your reader that two words, and sometimes more, go closely together. Their importance in report writing is to avoid ambiguity or conveying the wrong meaning. Fowler's *Modern English Usage* (2nd ed revised by Sir Ernest Gowers (1965) Oxford University Press, Oxford) offers as an example 'a little-used car'. If you leave out the hyphen the phrase means something completely different.

Many researchers leave out the hyphens because they do not know whether they should be there or not. Whether or not a word is hyphenated is often debatable because the language is constantly evolving. When two words become closely associated they go through three stages: of being separate, hyphenated and then one word, eg a hand down, hand-towel, handkerchief. There are two tips we can give you:

■　See whether leaving out the hyphen could alter the meaning of your phrase (as in the little used car example).

■　Look it up in the dictionary!

COLONS AND SEMI-COLONS

If you have trouble deciding when to use either of these punctuation marks or which you should use, then the best thing is probably to use neither and opt for a full stop. A semi-colon is something between a comma and a full-stop. If in doubt, make two sentences or put a conjunction such as 'and' between the two sentences. Colons have more definable uses. They are used mainly to separate a clause that introduces a list, a quotation, summary etc.

THE APOSTROPHE

Probably the most common punctuation error that pervades report writing is the incorrect use of 'its' and 'it's'. 'Its' without the apostrophe is possessive, the thing belonging to it, eg its colour, its size. With the apostrophe it means 'it is'.

Another common error is the use of the possessive when talking about things in the plural or using plural nouns. If you want to say the bricks belonging to the builders then you say the builders' bricks. If, on the other hand you want to say the bricks belonging to one builder, the apostrophe goes before the 's': the builder's bricks. The only tricky bit comes with plural nouns like people and children but you just treat them as if they were singular, eg the people's choice, the people's heroes.

THE IMPORTANCE OF PAYING ATTENTION TO DETAIL

A research report's credibility can be thrown into doubt if in the first chapter the figures do not add up, the brand names are spelt incorrectly, or, even worse, the client's name is wrong on the title page of the document. Although the report content and conclusions might be first class, the client can be left wondering what else has not been checked. It can also be the case that someone within the client company who does not like the research results or conclusions can use the errors to call into question the whole research project. The moral is: don't let stupid errors of detail in the report mar the success of a good piece of research.

There is nothing worse in a report than inconsistent spellings, headings, type-faces, etc. You should decide at the outset on which heading style, spelling, and so on you are going to use and stick to them throughout the report.

Also, you should take care to be consistent with facts. It is irritating, if not confusing, for the reader to read about a market size of £5m on one page and then, without explanation, find on the next page a table with contradictory figures.

CHECKING AND EDITING

When the manuscript is completed it must be read, corrected, and read and corrected once more. The author must take full responsibility for these two edits, the first looking for sense, logic and consistency and the second for accuracy and syntax. After the author's two edits is should be given to some other person whose role it will be to spot errors, *non sequiturs*, inconsistencies and lack of sense.

THE FIRST CHECK

If you have planned your report well in the first place then the overall structure should rarely have to be changed at the editing stage. However, there are times when it becomes clear that the report would flow better or would be easier to read if the chapters were moved round or sections moved into different chapters. You should be thinking all the time about what would make most sense to the readers.

The difficult part is editing the content. Once you have written something it becomes difficult to decide at the editing stage that it's irrelevant or wrong. However, at this stage you have to be brutal and apply the 'so what' rule rigorously. Does the point just made add to the client's knowledge and support the overall conclusions, or is it just there because you have the information?

THE SECOND CHECK

Here you should be checking:

- spelling
- grammar
- consistency
- that figures in tables and on diagrams add up correctly
- that table numbers follow in sequence.

There are now many checks built into word processing software packages. Spell checkers and a Thesaurus have been around for many years. A relatively new innovation is the grammar checker.[3] You first specify whether you are writing for business or informally and it will then check your document for spelling, punctuation, grammar, and style. For example, it will point out to you that you have started three sentences on the last page with the same wording and would you care to consider something different! While we are all for moving with the times we still feel that you should read and check a paper copy of your own report because:

- A simple spell checker can pick up spelling errors but not the context of the word. Therefore, it will not pick up 'their' instead of 'there'.
- What you see on screen is not always what you get on paper, eg the page breaks can be in the wrong place, the tabs out of line, etc.
- Seeing a paper copy may tell you that you have used too many verbatim comments, whereas this may not be so obvious a page at a time on the screen.

If time and budget permits, we would recommend that you ask a colleague to read your report. Indeed, many agencies now have Quality Systems such as BS 5750, which usually specify that a senior member of staff checks all reports. They are looking at it with a fresh eye and can often pick up points that you, being so close to the subject, have overlooked. However, their role should be as an editor and not a proof reader and the report should only be given to them when it has been through its two checks.

---

[3] For example, WordPerfect for Windows 6's *Grammartik*.

THE 30 PER CENT CHALLENGE

As the old saying goes: 'It's quality not quantity that counts'. Occasionally a client will not think he has got value for money unless the report is at least an inch thick but most of our clients hate wading through lengthy reports. There is little point writing 50 pages when 30 pages would do. It is a waste of time for both the writer and the reader.

The next time you write a report, particularly if you write it quickly without agonising over every line as you go along, try reducing it by a third while still keeping the sense. You will then get into the habit of doing this mentally before putting pen to paper or fingers to the keyboard.

7

MAKING THE REPORT LOOK GOOD

■

WHY MAKING THE REPORT LOOK GOOD IS IMPORTANT

They say you shouldn't judge a book by its cover but the overall appearance of a report does matter. A client may have paid a market research company tens of thousands of pounds for a report and it is not unreasonable to expect the report to be well presented. The physical production of the report is probably the most neglected area of the whole research process, perhaps for understandable reasons to the researcher but not to the recipient of the report. If considerable care is given to the production of presentation material, why is this not the case with reports? We think there is a very simple answer; the researcher has to use the presentation material him or herself. The researcher would be embarrassed putting up an acetate where the chart was crooked, or giving a presentation and finding that a slide was out of order or missing.

The report is often the last step in the research process, at which point the researcher is keen to move on to the next project. The minute the report has been checked, a sigh of relief goes up and far too often all responsibility for its production and despatch is abandoned. This is very short-sighted, as it is the report that will endure, whereas the presentation will be forgotten. Also, as the report may sit on a shelf for years, it is likely to be picked up by someone who was not at the presentation and they will judge the report on its own merits. Whether we like it or not, appearances count.

CONSIDERATIONS FOR REPORT PRODUCTION

There are two main aspects to report production that need to be considered:

■ Printing.
■ Materials.

There are no hard and fast rules about which materials to use, and what looks good or bad is often a matter of personal taste. Also, your influence over the materials used in report production may be limited if your organisation has its own house style that needs to be followed. However, rather than just accept the *status quo*, the points below may provoke some thought about how your system could be improved.

PRINTING

The word processor has provided us with a great opportunity to be creative when it comes to the appearance of the printed text. In one sentence we can mix point sizes, typefaces and styles. However, it is worth reiterating the point that your aim when report writing should be to communicate your findings in the clearest possible manner: too much variation can confuse rather than illuminate.

The most popular *typeface* for dense text in a smallish point size, is Times. The theory is that the serifs lead the eye from one letter to the next. Unless you want your report to be different for some reason, we would recommend sticking to a variation of the Times typeface. Other typefaces, such as Helvetica, are more suitable for large text, such as presentations.

The most popular *point size* for reports is 12. Use any larger and you may be accused of trying to make your report look longer than it really is. Use any smaller and you run the risk of complaints from those with failing eyesight.

Chapter *headings* should be in capitals and section headings in lower case. Whether you underline or embolden your headings is largely a matter of personal choice. When using headings within sections you should be consistent throughout the report. Also pay due regard to hierarchies; if your chapter heading is in bold upper case, do not use this elsewhere in the text or you could confuse your reader.

When *highlighting* or *emphasising* text by all means use any of the options open to you with modern word processing, such as double underlining, shadow, outline, etc but the principle is to be consistent. Italics are useful in three main ways:

- To pick out words for special emphasis.
- To pick out foreign words used singly or in short phrases in an English sentence.
- To refer to titles of books, magazines, etc.

The most important point about *page numbering* is that all reports should have it! Page numbers are probably best at the bottom of the page, either in the centre or on the right-hand side of the page.

A *margin* width of between 1–1½" is the accepted norm for reports. The main thing to ensure is that the text starts sufficiently far enough to the right for the reader to read, given the type of binding. There is nothing more frustrating than having to almost prise apart the report in order to be able to read the first word on every line.

With *line spacing* there are no set conventions for market research reports. It is a matter of looking at your page of printed text and deciding whether it looks too cramped or too sparse.

MATERIALS

There are three main factors which you need to take into consideration when choosing the materials to use:

■ Their appearance and the image you wish to project.
■ Their practicality and user-friendliness for the reader.
■ Their cost.

As a general rule you should use the best quality materials you can afford and which are appropriate to the importance of the report. For example, a short internal report with limited circulation will probably not justify expensive materials, whereas a major study with widespread distribution might merit printing special covers.

There are three choices to be made when it comes to the report *paper*:

■ Weight.
■ Finish (woven, vellum, etc).
■ Colour.

Copier paper is 80 gsm and is sometimes used for reports. However, a 100 gsm paper not only gives the report more of a quality feel, but also stands up better to use.

Using different colour paper in a report can be useful to differentiate between sections, for example the management summary or the questionnaires. This enables readers to locate easily the section they are seeking.

The purpose of the *cover* is to protect the report, to identify it and to project a certain image of the person or organisation producing it. Covers can be standard or customised for each report. Customised covers require advance planning and can be expensive but are worth considering for a particularly important report.

There are basically three *binding* systems in common use for market research reports, each of which have their pros and cons:

■ A slide system.
■ Spiral/comb binding.
■ Heat sealing.

Slide binders are practical for the report producer, as pages can easily be removed or added right up to the moment of despatch, and they look smart. They also require no special equipment, as the plastic binder is slipped over the report and covers by hand. However, they can make it difficult for the reader to keep the report open at the right place and there is a risk of pages working loose over time.

Spiral or *comb* binding is where a machine is used to punch perforations down the side of the pages and covers, through which a wire or plastic binder is inserted and thus the pages are held together. They are user-friendly for the reader provided that the correct size binder is used, ie not too tight. Their appearance is sometimes criticised, particularly when the binders are too big.

Heat sealing uses special equipment. The report pages are inserted into a book-like cover with adhesive inside. It is then put in a machine which melts the adhesive and sticks the pages together. Reports bound in this way look good provided that the pages are neatly aligned. The disadvantages are cost (a range of special covers of varying sizes needs to be purchased, whereas with slide and spiral binders the covers are the same irrespective of the thickness of the report), the risk of pages working loose and the difficulty of changing pages once the sealing process has taken place (although in theory this is claimed to be no problem).

CHECKLIST FOR REPORT PRODUCTION

Some of the tips below may seem too trivial or obvious to mention but most researchers will have fallen foul of at least one of them during the course of their careers.

■   Do not underestimate the time required for report production and checking. Even with the most sophisticated word processing and graphics systems, it still takes time to make sure the page breaks are in the right places, the tables are numbered consecutively, the table of contents is generated, etc. If you are dependent on someone else for typing or charts, do not assume that they will be available the minute you need them.

■ Although it is not always possible, try to ensure that you are not working up to the last minute. Computers, photocopiers and binders always choose the worst possible moments to break down.

■ If your client has requested a very large number of copies or you are using some special materials, make sure that the relevant stationery has been ordered in good time.

■ Check the printed reports for the following:
—That all the pages are included in the right order and there are no blank pages
—That the appendices are all there
—That charts on facing pages are in the right place
—That the printing is of an acceptable quality, ie not too faint, too dark, with lines or marks
—That the printing is straight.

■ Check that the covers and bindings are the ones you intended the report to have.

■ Consider how the reports should be delivered. Even if the report is for internal circulation, consider whether the internal mail system will deliver the report to the reader when promised. If you have worked all weekend to ensure that your client gets the report on time, don't take the chance of sending it by ordinary post. A client who has an important meeting at which the research findings will be discussed is hardly likely to be sympathetic to your plea of: '... but I posted it last night!'

PRESENTATIONS

8

COMMUNICATING WITH THE AUDIENCE

■

UNDERSTANDING THE AUDIENCE

It is self evident that a presentation cannot take place without an audience. Audiences for market research presentations are usually relatively small in number, perhaps between 3 and 10. If only a couple of people want to hear the findings then it would be more appropriate for the researcher to treat the presentation as a debrief, sitting down with the clients and talking them through the findings. Occasionally more than 10 people turn up to listen to a presentation, especially if the subject has solicited interest, but it is rare for market researchers to present findings to more than 30 people.

The chances are that even in a typical audience of around 10 people there will be different interests and levels of seniority. Market researchers may be present in the audience and they may be interested in the technicalities of the work and eager to know that all i's have been dotted and t's crossed. Marketing managers may have action to take as a result of the study and they will be less interested in the robustness of the data and want to hear more about where to go from here. Production and accounting staff will find the occasion useful for learning more about another aspect of the business, and also the implications, if the conclusions of the research change the plans of the factory and warehouse. For the Managing Director it may be an ideal chance to receive objective data on the business and also to be briefed on any strategic implications.

Different people, different interests, and different levels of seniority make life difficult for the researcher, as it may be impossible to pitch a presentation at a level that satisfies everyone. One approach is to defer to the most senior person but this could be inappropriate if, for example, the Managing Director only attends for educational reasons or to signify support for an issue, and not because of any direct involvement in further action. Flexibility must be built into the presentation so that an attempt can be made to meet the needs of most of the audience, keeping in mind those people to whom the results matter most. In the main, the people who matter most are those who will have to take action on the data when the presentation is over.

Audiences don't just materialise. Someone within a company is likely to be pivotal in the arrangement of the presentation and the researcher should find out from them who is due to attend. It can be helpful to find out a little about each member of the audience prior to the event. What are their main areas of interest? Why are they attending? What political corners may they be fighting? Being forewarned gives the researcher an opportunity to think about the questions that could be asked.

SEATING THE AUDIENCE

Sometimes the presenter has the opportunity to influence the seating arrangements of the audience. The two traditional layouts are 'board room style' and a 'U' or 'horseshoe' shape. Board room style is the most popular and here the audience sits around a large table or a number of tables pushed together. Chairs are laid out at the end and down the sides with one end left free for the presenter and the screen. The 'U' shaped arrangement is a variation on this theme but there is a space

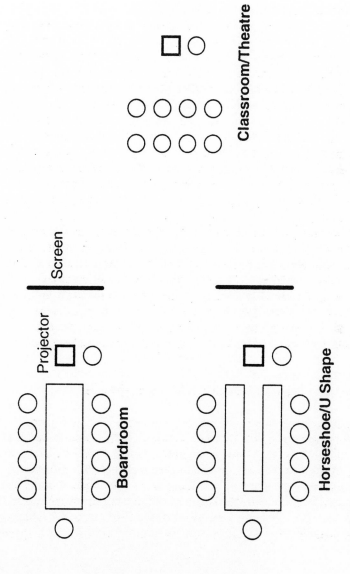

Figure 8.1 Different audience layouts

down the middle. These two arrangements are preferable to a classroom (or theatre) style made up of rows of seats. The classroom arrangement allows everyone to sit facing the presenter but it smacks of back-to-school with the presenter taking on the mantle of school teacher. Other disadvantages are that everyone has to turn around if there is a question from the back, people shy away from sitting on the front row and the presenter can suffer if there is a moat of empty chairs creating a physical barrier with the audience.

There are seldom fixed seating positions for individuals at presentations and people sit anywhere depending on their time of arrival, seniority and disposition to the research. Those arriving early and with a choice, may position themselves in seats that reflect their political stance. For example, antagonists are unlikely to sit close to the presenter, preferring to take a seat at the far end of the table so that from this safe distance they can sling their pointed questions. If people of opposite persuasions or conflicting personalities attend, they are likely to choose opposite sides of the table so that they can attack each other with the protection of a barrier. People who arrive late, those who are close to the research and friendly to the researcher and those who are relatively junior in status are likely to gravitate or be pushed into positions near the top of the table, closest to the presenter.

Even if the presenter has little opportunity to change the seating position of individuals, it can be useful to work out at an early stage who is sitting where just to be aware of where different types of questions could come from, so that steps can be taken to head off trouble by working especially hard on the troublesome groups, by using extra eye contact and rapport building.

As people settle down into their seats it is worthwhile making a rough plan, jotting down each person's name so that they can be addressed personally. In this regard, it is necessary to have a policy on how people will be addressed — by their first name or surname. In the main, market research presentations, like most business meetings, accept informal methods of address, even for those people who have just been introduced.

WHAT MAKES A GOOD PRESENTATION?

When all is said and done, it is of no concern what the researcher thinks of the presentation, it is the audience's view that matters. The researcher will very quickly obtain a feel for how things are going. Sympathetic nods and smiles from one or two people and encouraging questions are obvious signals that things are on the right track. Equally, drooping eyelids and bored or hostile expressions are a sure sign that they are not.

Clarity accepted, the audience wants to know what is in it for them — how is it relevant? The presentation should be able to answer the question: 'So what?' This means that audiences are looking for presentations that are short on descriptions and long on interpretation. They are looking for presentations that clarify complex situations and show a way forward. They are interested in solutions and not problems.

The individuals who were responsible for commissioning the work have a special requirement from the presentation. They have backed the researcher from the start and may well have fought for the researcher to be used on this project instead of on the salesforce, another research company or some other person. Now, at the finale of the study, the people who backed the researcher do not want to be let down. They will hope that their choice will be vindicated and will be as hopeful of a good performance as the researcher. From their point of view, a presentation is a good one if their colleagues say it is good.

Researchers face another hurdle in impressing their audiences. Though they may be reluctant to admit it, members of the audience are looking for stimulating ideas and, if only it were possible, an element of entertainment. They have given up their time to attend and hope to learn something that they can take away and to help build their business. They are also hoping that they will not be bored; that the presentation will be a pleasurable experience.

Some audiences contain aficionados of presentations. They have seen a large number of presentations and therefore have high standards by which to judge them. Media presentations such as those on television are viewed widely and help create

TABLE 8.1 WHAT MAKES A GOOD MARKET RESEARCH PRESENTATION?

	Total % mentioning	Market research managers % mentioning	Other management/ directors % mentioning
Clear, simple charts	52	42	56
Concise/to the point	26	30	24
Enthusiastic, knowledgeable presenter	23	27	21
Interpretation/ conclusions	21	21	21
Total	*	*	*
Sample size	100	33	67

*People mentioned several factors, therefore does not add up to 100.

expectations of such high standards. Furthermore, presentations look easy because the best presenters make them appear so. Therefore if they are so easy then it is expected that anyone can make them.

However, presentations are far from easy and if they appear so, it is simply because the best presenters are very experienced, almost certainly well practised and probably highly gifted. This means that a boffin researcher, a good researcher but one with his head in the clouds or lacking communication skills, faces a difficult task. The findings of the study may have been well worked out and the presentation could address the subject perfectly, but if it lacks sparkle, the event may be judged mediocre.

CONTROLLING THE AUDIENCE

There are a number of unwritten rules of etiquette that attendees of presentations observe. By and large people arrive on time, ask questions when it is signalled appropriate to do so, do not talk across the presenter and do not get up and leave in the middle without apologising. Occasionally these rules are broken, sometimes resulting in other members of the audience self-policing the situation. At other times, however, the presenter must intervene and is helped by the natural authority conferred by standing up and leading the show.

Question time needs most audience control. When to take questions needs deciding before the presentation begins. Formal presentations with large audiences are suited to a questions-and-answers session at the end. Very short presentations may also be better if the questions are saved to the end as in this circumstance they may interrupt the flow and pre-empt a point covered later. However, in long presentations, those which stretch for an hour or more, both the audience and the researcher require the welcome interruption of questions. For the researcher it is an opportunity to collect his or her thoughts. For the audience it is an opportunity to participate and make the whole affair more enjoyable. In a long presentation, questions would be forgotten and the momentum for asking them would be lost, so they should be encouraged as and when they arise.

Of course, presenters welcome easy questions as these provide the chance to demonstrate knowledge and satisfy the interest of the audience. However, not all questions are easy. People commissioning research have every right to challenge and dig to see if the results stand up to examination. Wrong information or an incorrect interpretation could result in a lost opportunity or considerable wasted expense. This is not to say that researchers will always cherish difficult questions but they must expect them and should not be resentful when they are raised.

Sometimes questions are loaded, the questioner hoping for an answer that can assist in some internal political scheming. Special vigilance is required with this type of question because at all costs it is necessary to remain demonstrably objective. This said, they are not always easy to spot. More usually, the clue comes from the person asking the question rather than the question itself.

Below are a number of tips for dealing with questions arising in a presentation:

■   Be happy to take questions and speak authoritatively when you answer. This will help build the audience's confidence in your replies.

■   In a similar vein, don't be afraid at any juncture of asking the audience what they think is the answer to a question. Someone may have a useful contribution to make and be happy to do so, without undermining the authority of your position or the standard of your work.

■   Look at the person who is asking the question when they are speaking. When you are answering, address the whole audience and conclude by looking at the questioner. This way you have the best chance of taking everyone with you.

■   If you are seeking a rapport with the audience and the presentation is likely to stretch over an hour, take command at an early point by throwing a question out to the audience.

■   Make sure that you understand the question and have fully thought about the answer. Don't interrupt while the question is being asked; not only is it impolite and you could miss the point, but you are also wasting valuable thinking time. Sometimes it can be helpful to ask for the question to be repeated or for you to re-state it so that it is clear that you truly understand it.

■   Without being patronising or trite, acknowledge a good question if it really is. Of course, 'a good question' can also be a euphemism for a difficult question or one that you cannot answer.

■ Be prepared to admit you don't know the answer to a question if that is the case. If you don't know the answer to a question don't pretend that you do, otherwise you will be exposed and lose credibility. Research isn't always perfect, nor can it always answer every question. Not everyone will be aware of the scope and limitations of the research and it is entirely reasonable that the greater knowledge obtained from the research has raised questions that cannot be answered without further research.

■ If you don't know the answer to a question but say that you could find it out given more time, make sure that you write the question down. You may forget later but it cannot be assumed that the questioner will.

■ Don't be imprecise and woolly with your answers. It is not helpful to give an answer that says on the one hand this, on the other hand the other. People are looking for firm guidance and you may have to present the contradicting pieces of information and conclude the answer with a firm opinion. However, it is important that you let the audience know what is fact and what is opinion.

■ Perhaps it is an obvious point but don't attempt to put down a questioner with a too-clever-by-half or cutting reply. If the questioner is being difficult then the chances are that someone else in the audience will do this for you. Don't get dragged into a gutter fight in a public arena as you will end up losing your authority, the audience's respect and your dignity.

9

DEVELOPING A STORY-LINE

■

WORKING OUT A STRONG THEME

'Let me tell you a story.' Those words still cause us to perk up in anticipation of something that will be pleasurable and interesting. Stories are what people want to hear and yet inevitably much of the information collected by market researchers is as dry as dust and impossible to present as some sort of yarn. Nor is it right to draw too close an analogy between stories and market research findings, as one is a fable and the other is carefully collected data. However, there are some aspects of story telling that can be used to enhance market research presentations. Good stories have a strong theme with an unfolding plot. In telling a story, personalities are developed and there are rich presentations of scenes. They have a beginning, a middle and an end. All these features can be lifted and used in presentations.

Whereas the report contains all the information, from a summary through to detailed findings, the presentation will be a shorter, sharper opportunity to communicate keynote findings. At an early stage the researcher should think about the theme for the presentation and the important issues to be communicated. The presentation is a golden opportunity to stimulate and interest an audience who may not have the time to read the report and who don't want to cover all the ground.

In the presentation, colour can be given to the findings and attention brought to the issues that matter most, which could get clouded in a long, written text. Whereas the conclusions and recommendations may occupy just 5–10 per cent of a report, they may account for a fifth of a presentation. People have turned up to learn, but more particularly to find out what it means to them and what they should do as a result.

KEEPING IDEAS SIMPLE

Inevitably, market research studies are heavy in findings. The very nature of the subject means that there will be a lot to say — even though the nervous researcher may feel short of information as the time for the presentation looms nearer. The trick is to break the data into manageable sections that the researcher can easily present and the audience can readily digest.

In order to make the presentation clear and memorable, it can be helpful to try to distil the subjects so that they are punched home with vigour. It is better to over-simplify than to over-complicate. Good presentations have just one, two or three themes that are set out at the beginning so that the audience can see the logic of what is being attempted. Within the framework of the theme or themes for the presentation there should be a beginning, a middle and an end. The beginning would be a brief description of the subjects on the agenda, the middle would be the meat of the findings and the end would comprise the conclusions.

One way of keeping things simple is to bunch ideas into groups: the mind has a handy knack of being able to remember things in multiples of threes. For example, a subject could be divided into three sections, perhaps looking at it from the point of view of the past, present and future or, alternatively, where a company is now, what it could achieve, and how it could achieve it. The 'rule of three' should not take over the structuring of the presentation but is mentioned as one means by which complex ideas can be reduced to simple, bite-sized chunks, assisting at one level in working out a clear story-line and at a detailed level in helping formulate clear and simple ideas for each slide.

LAYING OUT THE STRUCTURE FOR THE PRESENTATION

A maxim of presenting is to tell the audience what you are going to say, then say it, and finally remind them what you have just said. The logic behind this apparent repetition is that people like a quick plan and overview so that they can see what is coming. They then, of course, need to hear the detail and finally they need everything bringing together at the end in a succinct summary and conclusions. Slotted into this tried and tested method of communicating the findings will be the structure, which must now be worked out.

It is up to the researcher to decide exactly how the findings will be unfolded, not forgetting that there needs to be a link between sections and a clear direction without constantly having to spell it out. For example, a researcher looked at the opportunities for a supplier of domestic burglar alarms in France. The findings provided insights into the size, structure and trends in the market but there were no obvious gaps that a new supplier of alarms could fill. Setting up a company to market burglar alarms in France would bring the new operation into competition with existing suppliers and would take time and incur substantial costs. It would also be a risky option. A quick and safer route into the market would be by acquisition, though clearly this would be expensive and presupposes that there are companies for the taking. The theme of the presentation could centre on how to get into the French market for domestic burglar alarms and the story would be a build up to a recommended short list of companies which could be considered for acquisition. A presentation of this type could be covered in 40–45 minutes. A suggested structure would be as follows:

Slide 1	**Title**	Enabling the researcher to introduce the team and spell out the overall theme of the presentation — 1 minute
Slide 2	**Agenda**	Listing the subjects which will be covered in the presentation — 1 minute
Slide 3	**Objectives**	Summarising the objectives of the study and perhaps saying what it did *not* intend to achieve — 2 minutes
Slide 4	**Methods**	A quick statement of how the research was carried out — 2 minutes (note how short this section is)
Slide 5	**Definitions**	What constitutes the domestic intruder alarm market in France — 3 minutes
Slide 6	**Market size**	The first of the important findings showing how big the market is in France — 3 minutes
Slide 7	**Segments**	How the market breaks down into its various component parts (eg specifier groups, product segmentations etc) — 3 minutes
Slide 8	**Distribution**	Routes by which burglar alarm products move through the market from manufacturer to buyer — 4 minutes
Slide 9	**Prices**	Prices, margins and discounts at different levels in the distribution chain — 3 minutes
Slide 10	**Suppliers**	The different suppliers of burglar alarms and their shares, together with comment on their strengths and weaknesses — 7 minutes
Slide 11	**Trends**	Where the market has come from and where it is going in the future, explaining what is driving the market growth, and any technological changes — 5 minutes

Slide 12 **Options**	The pros and cons of entering the market by setting up a new operation or making an acquisition — 5 minutes
Slide 13 **Recommendations**	The next steps — 5 minutes

The dozen or so acetates which have been outlined for this 40 minute presentation is not a magical figure and indeed there is a justification for having more than one acetate to cover the subject of 'suppliers' and 'options' where it was intended to talk for five minutes or more. Around 15 to 20 acetates would have been the right number.

Of course, if the presentation is required to last longer, each of the subject areas could be opened up and would become a sub-section with its own set of acetates. It is not to be recommended but sometimes the researcher has no choice and is booked in to give a presentation of two or three hours. In such circumstances the same logical structure could be used but it would be necessary to increase the number of acetates on each topic. In most presentations three to five minutes per acetate is sufficient. In seminar type presentations lasting over an hour, the audience will be deeply involved in the discussion and a single acetate could sit on the screen for up to ten minutes.

SPECIAL REQUIREMENTS OF QUALITATIVE RESEARCH

Group discussions and depth interviews generate ideas and messages that cannot be tabulated or graphed. The insights obtained from qualitative research are very personal to the person who moderated the groups or carried out the depth interviews, and it is difficult for anyone else to pick up these nuances and make a credible presentation. This contrasts with quantitative research which generates facts and figures, which almost any competent researcher can interpret and present.

The qualitative researcher still must find a theme for the presentation and here there is room for imagination. A researcher carried out qualitative research among buyers of new homes and was struck by how the whole process seemed like a game of chance. Pitfalls awaited the new house buyers

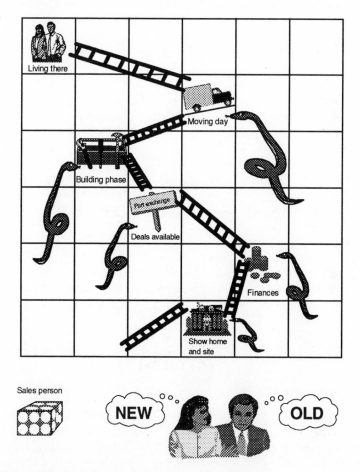

Figure 9.1 A game of chance for house buyers

everywhere but at every stage a good sales negotiator (the person on the site who actually sells the house) could smooth them over. The researcher decided to set the theme of the presentation around a snakes and ladders board, showing how the house buyers moved from level to level (or fell down snakes) until the day they moved in. The sales negotiator was represented as a dice with a throw of six indicating the luck of finding someone who was really good, as they would help the move onwards and upwards. The image projected by this metaphor was very strong and provided an early framework for the presentation and a lead into the subjects of looking around for a house, deciding which one to choose, organising the finance, waiting for the transaction to go through, moving in, etc. The graphic of the snakes and ladders board gave a quick and early insight into the whole process and provided the link to the sub-sections where the findings could be discussed in more detail.

In qualitative research it is necessary to communicate what people said, why they said it and what it means. Answers to what people have said can be stated as bullet points or more powerfully as direct quotes. These have all the more impact

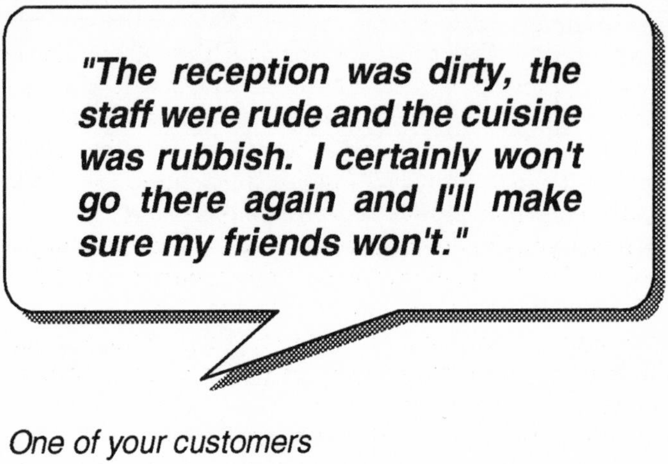

"The reception was dirty, the staff were rude and the cuisine was rubbish. I certainly won't go there again and I'll make sure my friends won't."

One of your customers

Figure 9.2 Use direct quotes for impact

because they are seen to be points made by customers or potential customers and they are not the words of the researcher. Of course, this makes it all the more important that the researcher is careful in the selection of the quotes, ensuring that they are truly representative and not fringe comments chosen to support the researcher's prejudices.

MAKING THE STORY INTERESTING

With the best will in the world it may be impossible to jazz up a mundane market research study and, in any case, to do so may offend the audience by appearing to trivialise a subject that is the kernel of their business interest. The market research may yield predictable and uninspiring results, though again it is important not to prejudge the findings. As uninspiring as they might appear to the researcher, they could be fascinating to a client whose business is built on the subject. Even taking this positive view, there will still be times when a presenter can see that the subject is dry and the audience is flagging. Long presentations, those which take place after lunch and those with large doses of statistical information can all be heavy going and need enlivening.

It is important that the story begins with a strong line and engages the audience's interest from the start. At this time the audience will be at their most attentive. The presentation is just beginning and they will be settling down, watching the presenter and making snap decisions on what the presentation will be like. A good start will create the right first impressions.

Whatever you do, do not begin the presentation with any sort of apology for the quality of your presentation material or the data. You may draw attention to something that would not be noticed but your apologetic manner may begin to sow seeds of doubt about the overall quality of the research. The only time to apologise is if you are late.

This may be one of the few occasions in the whole presentation when it is worth remembering a few lines, just to kick-start the flow of words to come, once the vocal chords are warmed up and everything has settled down. Some suggestions for starting a presentation are:

- A brief biographical note, introducing yourself, what you do and the department or company for which you work.
- A quote which relates to the theme of the presentation.
- An anecdote about the study, which provides a lead into the story.
- A brief record of the events that led up to the research being commissioned.

Humour can be used to make the story interesting but should be treated carefully. Unless the presenter is an accomplished raconteur, there is a danger that a joke will fall flat and leave everyone feeling embarrassed. The safest jokes, if they are to be made at all, should be against the presenter. However, it is still wise not to push them too far; the aim being to waken up an audience, obtain a smile and build rapport and not to have them rolling in the aisles. More acceptable than the joke is a light-hearted story connected to the research; something a respondent said, a practical example, or a comparison with another market and another piece of research. These stories build character into the presentation but, just as humour can be difficult to handle, care is required because a badly-selected example may appear off-key or patronising to the audience. Despite these cautionary notes, it is better for people to get excited because the presenter chose a wacky role model to explain something, rather than allowing everyone to drift into semi-consciousness and not take in a word of what has been said.

People have a tolerance of around five to ten minutes before their interest begins to wane. Try to seed the presentation with anecdotes or issues that add texture and build interest. Motivational issues have a high interest quotient; in certain markets an interesting subject could be environmental issues or pressures that are changing the market. If these high interest subjects are introduced at intervals during the presentation they will provide the presenter with something to be more passionate about and this very enthusiasm will ensure that the story becomes more interesting and persuasive.

It is important to keep a constant watch on the audience for feedback. It will be perfectly clear if the story is boring and, if they are bored, it will not be what is said but how it is said, so emphasising the importance of rapport building techniques, which are discussed in Chapter 8.

In the same way that the start of the presentation is crucial, it is important to finish strongly and not leave the audience feeling flat. As the presentation comes to an end, the researcher will feel relief, even exhaustion, and the drive to remain involved in the subject may be low. Just as an athlete runs to a distance, so the researcher feels that the job is now over. Far from it; the finishing line has not been crossed yet because from the research sponsor's point of view, they are only just about to get to grips with using it. Questions will arise, not only during the presentation, but subsequently as the work is gradually absorbed. One way of concluding the presentation is to acknowledge that the job is nearly, but not quite, over and that some words are required so that the researcher can hand back to the audience, to the chairman or simply ask people to break for coffee. It is worth working out these concluding sentences in advance, such as: 'Thank you for your attention. I hope that you have enjoyed listening to my findings as much as I have enjoyed telling you about them. It is a big subject and no doubt you have some questions, which I welcome.' Or: 'Ladies and gentleman, thank you for your interest. I know that from my point of view I am almost at the end of my part of the exercise and you are just about to pick it up. I leave you with a copy of the slides and a report will follow shortly. Questions are sure to arise as you digest the findings so please contact me at any time and I will do my best to answer them.'

HOW TO REMEMBER THE STORY

Capturing information in the written word is difficult enough; there is a lot to say and the order in which it is said, the detail given and the way the story is told will determine its success. It is even more difficult to communicate the same information verbally, standing up, feeling nervous and trying to sound and look authoritative.

Presenters differ in the way they remember a story. First it must be said that all presenters spend a considerable length of time soaking themselves in the subject, not learning the lines by rote but thinking about what they want to say. Some make notes on the leaves of paper that separate the acetates, others prefer a separate sheaf of notes or cards in their hand. Some go so far as to write out everything they want to say and have it before them, not to read out (that would be sure to send people to sleep) but for personal comfort and confidence. The old stagers, those who are used to coping with their nerves and are experienced at giving presentations, are able to use the bullets and images on the acetates as prompts for recalling the story.

For the researcher who is new to presenting there is only one way to make sure that they are on top of the subject and that is to practise, practise and practise. It is hard to replicate the atmosphere of the day of the presentation but dummy runs do help drum in messages and, like revision for exams, boost confidence in that everything possible has been done. When practising, it is beneficial to stand up as this will be the posture on the day. Also, standing helps in other ways by sharpening the mind and providing the opportunity to experience and control body movements. Time each of the practice sessions but be aware of the fact that in reality it will take longer, it always does. If possible, arrange a presentation to friends and colleagues. This will be a closer replication of what it will feel like on the day with people to look at and offer feedback.

In the space of 45 minutes a presenter will deliver 3–4000 words, which are spontaneously constructed on the spot. There is bound to be some repetition of words, some stumbling and a few uhms and ahs. The presentation will have only a third or a quarter of the words contained in the report and, by contrast, the report will be tightly scripted without any repetition. This means that the researcher cannot be expected to say everything that is contained in the report and must concentrate on the highlights. It is inevitable that there will be some things, almost always small points, that the researcher intends to mention but forgets to do so in the heat of the moment. This is not something to lose sleep about because undoubtedly the crucial issues will have been communicated.

10

USING VISUAL AIDS

■

THE POWER OF WHAT IS SEEN AND HEARD

That which is seen is remembered much longer than that which is simply heard while that which is both seen and heard is remembered longest. A presentation supported by strong visual aids adds emphasis to points, brings clarity to what is being said and makes everything more interesting and memorable. However, visual aids are, as the name suggests, just aids and should not take over the whole show. There is a danger that researchers, new to presenting, will find comfort hiding behind their visual aids, hoping that they will distract the attention from themselves in their misery. The researcher should not lose sight of the fact that presentations depend mainly on the presenter and that visual aids are 'nice to have' but are by no means essential.

Dependency on visual aids can be a bad thing and many a well prepared presentation has been thrown into disarray by a technical hitch that has prevented their use. A market researcher once went to deliver a lecture at an Eastern European university. Diligent to a point, the researcher checked that there would be an overhead projector. On the due date the researcher arrived to present the lecture, which was woven around a pile of stunning coloured acetates. The overhead projector was there as requested, complete with a working bulb, but unfortunately there was no screen and every wall was a deep shade of brown. The slides had to be abandoned and the researcher was left to manage as best he could with chalk and talk.

The term visual aids, to most market researchers, means acetates. However, there will be occasions where other types of aids are useful and these range from 35mm slides to white boards and flip charts, video clips and demonstrations or handouts of products. In this chapter we discuss each type of visual aid showing when, where and how to use them.

THE FUNCTION OF VISUAL AIDS

We have argued that visual aids increase the impact of a presentation as they reinforce the spoken word. They also offer structure, interest and are a useful means of leaving a summary of the findings.

VISUAL AIDS PROVIDE A STRUCTURE FOR A PRESENTATION

A presentation needs a strong-story line; a clear thread which takes the audience through the findings. Designing the presentation within the framework of the visual aids can provide that thread. Each chart gives the presenter a cue and some notations on which to expand. The charts drive the story, ensuring that it is presented in a clear and logical manner. In this way the researcher can present the findings without notes, hanging the story around the bullet points and graphics on the charts.

VISUAL AIDS ADD INTEREST TO THE PRESENTATION

A chart is made up of text, pictures or diagrams and these add interest to what is being said. Moreover, the expectation of another chart can keep the attention of the audience as each is introduced and a fresh point is made. On the other hand, the researcher who enters a room and thumps a three inch pile of acetates next to the projector, will cause many a heart in the audience to sink. Too many charts signal a presentation that is likely to go on for too long.

VISUAL AIDS PROVIDE A SUMMARY OF THE FINDINGS

It can be helpful to present the findings of a study shortly before the publication of the report. This phasing of the delivery of the report gives the researcher the opportunity to integrate points raised in the presentation. In the meantime, the sponsor of the research is left with a hand-out of the slides, which provides a suitable summary of the findings. Presentation hand-outs are often the document that many commissioners of research use on a daily basis, as they are easier to flip through and yet contain all the salient data.

ACETATES/OVERHEADS/TRANSPARENCIES

WHEN AND WHERE TO USE ACETATES

Acetates are very easy to produce. Every photocopier can reproduce a paper chart on to an acetate (also known as an 'overhead' or 'transparency') which can then be projected by an epidiascope (more commonly referred to as an overhead projector) on to a screen. The cost of each acetate is relatively modest at around 50p. The original 'artwork' for the chart can be produced easily on word processing packages, computer graphics packages or by copying text and diagrams from brochures and journals. Creating the charts and the subsequent acetates is simple, quick and inexpensive — all important to the market researcher working to a tight timetable and budget.

Overhead transparencies work best for presentations aimed at audiences of 30–40 people. Beyond this number the chances are that people at the back of the room will find a conventional screen hard to see.

Researchers make transparencies 'work hard' for them by loading them with more information than would be the case in a 35mm slide. This is not an excuse to simply copy pages from reports on to acetates or even to produce very wordy slides. However, an overhead transparency will, if necessary, work with as many as 50 words, which is more than double the number that is advisable on a 35mm slide.

The precise talking time allocated to each acetate will vary; some being the subject of as little as a few seconds, with others taking 10 minutes or more. As a guideline, a typical 45 minute presentation requires 20–25 acetates, averaging out at two to three minutes per slide.

An important advantage of an overhead projector is the ability to make the presentation without totally darkening the room; essential in the case of 35mm slides. Even with dimmed lights, it is possible for the audience to make notes and to see the presenter and other people in the audience. This allows the researcher to maintain the high ground and keep the acetates in their rightful place as aids and only that. In a totally darkened room there would be more focus on the visual aids and less opportunity for the presenter to hold the audience's attention for a long time on each slide.

WORKING WITH OVERHEAD PROJECTORS

Most overhead projectors follow a standard format, which comprises a simple light box with mirrors and lenses. Light is thrown upwards from a mirror through a magnifying glass on which sits the slide. The image is then reflected via a mirror and lens at the end of a 'swan neck' on to the screen. Before making the presentation it is worth cleaning the build up of dust from the glass platen and the lens at the top of the swan neck. This may significantly increase the lumens and therefore improve the quality of the slide reproduction.

The bulb in the light box glows hot and is cooled by a fan. Heat and jolting of the projector takes its toll and the bulbs are prone to failure. Thus, as a precaution, many projectors have a second bulb that can be slid into place as needed. Of course, the last person using the projector may have faced a failure in the primary bulb, used the back-up and not replaced the original, so it is wise to confirm the availability of a spare bulb at the time the projector is booked.

Before the presentation begins, the overhead projector should be brought into focus. This may involve more than just altering the height of the mirror and lens. The screen should be tilted slightly forwards at the top to achieve a square image and reduce any keying effect. This pre-presentation check should also ensure that the projector and screen are correctly positioned so that both the top and bottom of each slide is visible to all parts of the audience.

The size of the room, the layout of the furniture, the light from the windows and the number of people in the audience will all influence where the screen and projector should be positioned. Conventionally the screen and projector stand square at the end of the room so that the people sat around the three sides of a rectangular arrangement are treated equally. Of course, the presenter has to stand alongside the projector and is, therefore, in danger of blocking the view of people close to the front. Using a little thought, the presenter will be able to step back from the projector and stand alongside the screen so that nobody's view is obstructed. Alternatively, the screen could be moved into the corner so that the presenter can stand in the centre of the room and not hinder anyone's view, though with this layout the people along the projector side of the table are disadvantaged and will have to crane their necks.

USING OVERHEAD TRANSPARENCIES

In many respects overhead transparencies are simple to use since, in principle, all that is necessary is that they are laid on a lighted projector. Below are some tips which will ensure that this most simple tool of presentation is used still more effectively.

■ Refer to the acetate. Place the acetate on the projector when it is needed and not before and refer to everything on it. Don't leave a slide on the screen if the discussion has moved on. If there is no appropriate slide for use while a point is being made, turn the overhead projector off so as to bring the attention back to the presenter. However, don't flick the projector on and off each and every time a new slide is shown as this is unnecessary and will soon agitate the audience.

■ Don't read out every word on the acetate. The audience are quite capable of reading the words themselves. If the chart contains a series of quotes, give the audience time to read them by reading them silently yourself. Instead of regurgitating what is on the slide, point out what it means.

■ Be prepared to dump acetates. Just because you have 40 acetates doesn't mean you have to use every one. If you sense that the point has been covered, is not relevant or that time is running out, set the slide to one side and move on.

■ Keep the acetates clean. Greasy finger marks will show up on the screen so make sure that your hands are clean and dry when handling acetates and try to touch them only around the edge.

■ Ensure that the acetates are positioned four square every time. It can be annoying to the audience if every slide is positioned skewwhiff, requiring later adjustment so that it is square on the screen. Overhead projectors have small locating lugs around the sides and these can be twisted to make them stand proud. An acetate pushed up against the lugs will always be in position.

■ Face the audience not the screen. It is a temptation to look at the screen for the prompts on what to say. Try to memorise what is on the slide or stand next to the projector and look down at the slide on the platen and back up to the audience rather than turning away all the time.

■ Point to the screen. Often a finger is as good a pointer as anything, except when the screen is large and parts of it are out of reach, in which case use a retractable 'aerial' type pointer. Alternatively a pencil laid on the acetate will throw a shadow on the screen in the form of a pointer.

■ Reveal bullets on an acetate but be careful. Sometimes a presenter wants to disclose points one by one, keeping the focus on each until ready to move on. This is easily done by placing a sheet of paper over the acetate and dragging it down to expose the next point. (Note that the paper is less likely to fall off if it is placed *under* the acetate.) As with all techniques of presenting using overheads, disclosure should not be over played as the audience may soon begin to feel that they are being controlled and considered incapable of looking at a complete slide.

■ Be prepared to use a marker pen. Acetates are made for writing on with special pens. Emphasis can be achieved by crossing something out, circling or underlining with the pen.

■ Don't fidget. When using an overhead projector the presenter is still the focus of the audience's attention. The audience will accept almost anything from a presenter as long as it is done naturally and without affectation. Little things don't matter if they are done just once but if they are repeated for an hour they become very noticeable and get on one's nerves. Constantly opening and closing a ring binder to take out the next slide will eventually become annoying. Similarly, a presenter who fusses constantly with the focus, or who is forever straightening slightly cockeyed slides, will soon begin to irritate.

■ Place the used acetates in a neat pile. Before the presentation begins, decide where you will place your discarded acetates and as they are used, put them there, don't scatter them around or drop them on the floor. Not only will it look neater and more organised to the audience, it will make the tidying up process easier when you have finished. And, you never know when you will need them again because if the presentation is a good one, you may be asked to give a repeat performance!

MAKING OVERHEAD TRANSPARENCIES

Colour and graphic images brighten up acetates but the time required to add these touches can be quite considerable. Whether or not this expense is justified depends on the job. A small project with a low budget may not justify a fancy presentation and the effort may be better spent on data collection and interpretation.

It is difficult to give clear-cut guidance as to who should be responsible for the creation of the charts. For someone who knows their way around one of the graphic packages such as *Harvard Graphics, Freelance, DrawPerfect, Pagemaker* and the like, it can be as quick to create them on screen as to sketch them by hand. However, the skills required to make the most use of all the features of a graphics package can take a long time to acquire, and the learning doesn't stop here. Supplementary to the graphic packages are libraries of clip art, which can enhance charts but again these take some time to get to know.

Researchers who are not fully *au fait* with the graphic systems can while away many a happy hour creating their charts when they would be better occupied doing something else. Chart creation can be a pleasant diversion and far easier than some of the tougher but more essential tasks in the research process. On the other hand, the only way to become skilled in chart production is to have a go. As always the answer must be some sort of balance, as some people will find that they have an interest and aptitude for creating charts while others prefer to delegate the work.

If a company has a sufficient demand for charts, it could be worthwhile having someone who specialises and so becomes adept in their production. Whether charts are produced by the researcher or a specialist chartist is very much something that must be worked out as being right for the employee and the company that employs them.

Consistency is important in the slide presentation, whether acetates or 35mm, and gives a theme and an air of professionalism to the whole presentation. Tips here include:

- Using standard formats for each slide. Graphics packages offer a variety of borders that can be used to frame each slide. The borders should be tasteful and appropriate to the subject. Colour themes can be used to indicate a change in section, though as always, simplicity should always win over the elaborate.
- As far as possible have all the slides portrait or landscape. Landscape slides look best and do not need rejigging on the platen so that the audience can see what is on the bottom. However, sometimes long tables cannot be accommodated on landscape formats and this dictates the alignment for the rest of the slides.
- Use simple typefaces. Overhead transparencies work well with a clean, unfussy typeface such as Helvetica or Times. Fonts should be large; around 22 point bold works well for headings and 15 point for text. Don't mix typefaces as they will make the slide appear messy.

35MM SLIDES

WHEN AND WHERE TO USE 35MM SLIDES

35mm slides are used when presenting to large audiences or projects where a very high impact presentation is required.

35mm slides require a room to be darkened to be effective. The slides are loaded into a carousel or magazine and moved backwards or forwards by means of a remote button activated by the presenter. The quality of the reproduction of 35mm slides is superior to those used on overhead projectors but they cost much more. Usually the slides need to be made by a graphics company that has the appropriate cameras, processing facilities and software to create 3D effects and backgrounds of every hue and colour. The cost can range from £15–25 per slide, depending on the complexity and the number required.

A 35mm slide can be held on the screen for much less time than an overhead. Far fewer words should be used on a 35mm slide, a handful being the ideal and 20 or 30 the absolute maximum. Bullet points are added one at a time using as many slides as there are bullets. A 35mm slide is on the screen for an average of just 30 seconds, which means that a half hour presentation will require 60 slides, perhaps costing more than £1000 in visual aids. Only those market research projects which demand an 'all singing, all dancing' presentation can justify this type of expense.

CHECKING OUT THE TECHNOLOGY OF 35MM PROJECTORS

35mm slides are almost always presented with the screen square to the audience. The screen can be positioned relatively high in the room so that the presenter is able to find somewhere to stand or sit, which does not block any views. It is especially important to check out the equipment to ensure that the carousel or magazine is compatible with the projector and that the presenter knows which button to press to go forward or back and how to alter the focus quickly and efficiently. Not least the researcher needs to run quickly through all the slides before the presentation to make sure that they are in order and facing the right way.

USING 35MM SLIDES

In one respect using 35mm slides is even easier than using overheads. In the dark all the attention is removed from the presenter and focused on the slide. All the researcher has to do is get across the story, moving progressively through the slides. The sequence of the slides organises the presentation but so too reduces its flexibility. The facility for skipping back to earlier slides or withdrawing slides that have become superfluous is severely restricted. It is not as easy to take questions *during* a 35mm presentation; for one thing the questioner is not visible and secondly the question tends to break the flow of the carefully structured story. Nor is it easy for members of the audience to take notes, and hand-outs of the slides are expensive to prepare.

All these disadvantages seem to indicate that 35mm slides are a poor means of presentation. However, for the big and formal occasions, when it is necessary to achieve a considerable impact, 35mm slides are much superior to acetates. It is for this reason that the Market Research Society insists that all its speakers at the annual conference present using 35mm slides.

MAKING 35MM SLIDES

Making 35mm slides takes time and requires care. The slides have to be sketched out and given to the graphics company, who will usually ask for a few days to turn them round. Then, if there are any mistakes or additions, the new or modified slides must be regenerated, and again a day or two is required. It is expedient to allow around a week for the whole process, a timescale that must be set against the couple of hours required to make acetates for a presentation of a similar length.

FLIP CHARTS AND WHITEBOARDS

Flip charts and whiteboards are not used to present the findings of complete surveys, but they are effective for amplifying or supporting subjects. Flip charts have the advantage of allowing the researcher to extemporise and adjust the presentation to the needs of the audience. Powerful points can be conveyed on flip charts or whiteboards even when the presenter's writing isn't the neatest in the world and the sketches aren't perfect. The very act of writing or drawing something on the chart helps the audience remember what has been said as it is written into their minds.

In certain circumstances the use of a flip chart or board may be patronising to an audience. In order to use the chart the researcher has to turn away from the audience and reduces the audience to the status of students. On these grounds flip charts are best used to add emphasis and to answer points when presenting findings and their extensive use is best confined to training sessions and briefings.

VIDEO AND AUDIO CLIPS

The use of video film can be dramatic in a presentation. A video clip does not need to be long; three to five minutes on a particular issue will be sufficient to communicate powerful messages. It could, for example, feature comments from a group discussion, show respondents at a hall test, or cover a visit to a shop or trade counter. The video has special power for capturing attention because it is a dynamic medium and relatively novel in presentations.

Finding the right words from metres of original film takes time. Making a compilation tape of bits and pieces of film takes even longer, involving locating and splicing together appropriate comments and scenes. And with the best will in the world the quality of the film is likely to be amateurish. Videos made at group discussions are shot from fixed positions and do not pan the room or close in on people who are speaking. Ordinary people have poor diction, speak softly or do not look to camera and so the results are unlikely to be professional.

Bearing all these points in mind about video clips, the only other thing to ensure is that the necessary equipment will be available for the presentation, and is suitable for VHS film.

Finding the right bits of an audio tape made in a group discussion can also take hours to put together and even then the speech may be indistinct. It could be better to have 'actors' (more likely colleagues at work) read from transcripts of the groups so that a clearer representation can be achieved.

COMPUTER SCREEN PRESENTATIONS

Nearly all computer graphics packages have facilities for generating presentations on the computer itself. While this may be acceptable for a debrief to three or four people, a presentation to a larger audience would need the images to be projected through a small piece of electronic wizardry on to a conventional screen.

Computerised presentations will almost certainly become more important in the future, as they obviate the creation of acetates or 35mm slides, and so offer advantages of speed and cost. On the other hand, projected images from a computer require special equipment and presenters must be more than researchers, feeling at home with the technology, or else requiring the assistance of a technician. To this extent they lack the simplicity of a conventional presentation using acetates.

PRODUCTS AND HAND-OUTS

There is nothing like passing around a product or a photograph during a presentation to capture attention. Products are tactile. Even when people are familiar with products, they like to pick them up for examination. Other items that engage interest are adverts, sales literature of companies and samples. Be prepared for the passing around of products to be a diversion, to create discussion and possibly to cause a temporary break in the proceedings.

11

COPING ON THE DAY

■

NERVES ARE ALL IN THE MIND

As a child, have you ever walked along a 3" wide kerb pretending that there was a 1000 foot drop on either side? In this fantasy you are able to keep perfect balance, swivel around, jump up and down and do all manner of tricks. If the fantasy were ever to become a reality and it was necessary to walk along a 3" track with a real 1000 foot drop on either side, your reaction would be very different. The width of the walkway would be the same but you would struggle to keep your balance and pirouetting would be impossible.

Now think about some of the occasions when you wax lyrical on your favourite subject in front of good friends. You are fluent, your ideas flow readily, you are totally relaxed but forceful and enthusiastic with your arguments. If we could imagine that as you were talking you were whisked, without realising it, on to a stage facing an array of microphones and 30,000 people, what would be your reaction? Setting aside that we cannot physically arrange this little experiment, it would be fair to say that the new situation would cause your fluency to dry up, your relaxed state to turn to panic and anxiety and that your mind could freeze up. The environment in which we are placed plays tricks with our *stimulus control* and learning to cope in presentations requires us to learn how to control the stimuli and not let them control us.

We respond to an environmental situation and all the stimuli it provides because we have *learned* to do so. We know that when we are walking along the 3" kerb that it is really a game and that there isn't a 1000 foot drop either side, even though we may be pretending that there is. If there really was such a drop our mind would tell us that this was for real and the physical reaction would change accordingly. We learn from an early age that heights mean hard falls and so, if we were faced with a 1000 foot drop, all the stimuli would be very negative.

The first time we have to speak before a group of people who we do not know, on a subject we are unsure about, it is a new experience and it is to be expected that we will feel nervous. This is a learning experience and is followed by reinforcements that sometimes can be negative or positive. The way that it goes will influence our future feelings and behaviour. If the first presentation is a good one, there will no doubt be much praise and a consequent feeling of well-being. This positive reinforcement satisfies the hunger for an ego boost and encourages the desire to repeat the exercise. However, if it goes badly, it will reinforce the negative aspects of carrying out presentations, so that the next time the occasion arises there is fear and dread.

Let us imagine you are asked to make a presentation to a board of directors about a market research project on which you have been working for a couple of months. You know your subject as well as anyone could. You are well rehearsed but unsure about your ability to present to such a senior group of people because you have never done so before. On the big day you are tense knowing the enormity of the occasion and having been wound up by colleagues who stop by to ask how you feel. You enter the board room, a totally unfamiliar environment, and are faced by a sea of faces that looks expectantly towards you. As you stand at the overhead projector you are gripped by a feeling of panic and a violent physical reaction wells up. Your pulse races, your breathing becomes more rapid, your legs begin to tremble and your mouth goes dry. Your hands shake and your voice moves into tremolo. You stumble through the presentation not enjoying one second of it. Eventually, after what seems like an age, you are through and disappear to your office where you feel humiliated and depressed. You doubt that you will ever be able to make a presentation again and certainly will make sure you avoid doing so if only you can.

During the presentation there was a feeling of being out of control. In fact things were out of control and the *autonomic nervous system* had taken over. Sweating, blushing and voice tremors were all manifestations which arose automatically. These things happen if the negative reinforcers beat the positive ones.

Now imagine that within a short space of time an opportunity occurs to make another presentation but, since you are still recoiling from the trauma of the previous occasion, you devise an excuse and someone else does it for you. The sense of relief is enormous and your failure to make the presentation is rewarded by a feeling of well-being through not doing it. In this way you are creating a set of circumstances which encourages you not to make presentations as the reward is the feeling of relief.

Let us move now to your armchair at home where you sit completely relaxed with no worries. You are asked to project yourself into another presentation. You are told to picture yourself once again in front of the board and that you are being questioned aggressively about your research findings. Just thinking about this situation is likely to be sufficient to induce sweating of the palms and an anxious feeling. And while it is possible easily to think oneself into such a situation, it is more difficult to think oneself out of it. The mind is gripped by all the reasons why the next presentation will be a repeat performance of the previous disaster and this becomes a self-fulfilling prophesy or else every opportunity is taken to make sure that you are never put in a position where you have to give another presentation.

We have all suffered similar reactions to presentations, not knowing how to overcome them and hoping that it is a simple matter of applying a number of tips that will enable us to break out and improve. Certainly, there are isolated tips which improve the quality of a presentation but first and foremost we must get a grip on our nerves. This means we must understand the way our nerves work so that we know why we feel like we do and how we can create positive reinforcers, which enable us to make a confident delivery.

THE POSITIVE SIDE OF NERVES

At the time you stand quaking before an audience, or as you recall the negative stimuli which you experienced at your last presentation, you may strongly dispute the assertion that nerves can be a positive thing. However, your nerves are an essential part of a good presentation and harnessing them is fundamental to success. The changes that occur when the sympathetic part of the nervous systems takes over prepare our body for a massive increase in activity. We are no longer tired. The mind is sharpened and enables us to think quickly and clearly. In fact the change brings an enthusiasm to our delivery that may be lacking if we were too relaxed and so it is to be encouraged.

Also, it should be recognised that the nerves never go away. The very best presenters nearly always suffer a bout of nerves before they begin but they are able to use it in a positive and creative way. Managing your nerves and making sure that you are in control is a vital part of presenting. So, the starting point is to recognise that nerves are natural, that everyone suffers them, but that they will work for you, not against you, if you know how to manage them.

MANAGING YOUR NERVES

Our autonomic nervous systems are made up of two opposing sub-departments; the *sympathetic* part, which churns us up so that we can cope with the stress that is about to occur and the *parasympathetic* part, which calms us down. In our normal state these two are in equilibrium providing enough get-up-and-go to do the job but not so much that we wear ourselves out through nervous exhaustion. However, when we are called upon to make a presentation, the sympathetic side takes over and pours

Negative and positive stimuli affect the autonomic nervous system

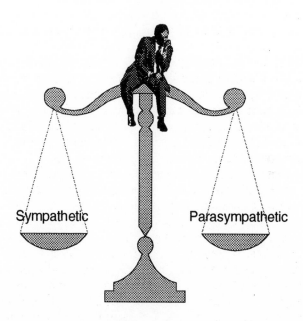

Figure 11.1 Nerves in fine balance

adrenalin into the blood. A chemical change occurs within the body; the heart beats faster, blood rushes to the face and neck, the digestive process is slowed down, carbohydrate in the liver sends the blood sugar soaring, breathing becomes quicker and we start to sweat.

In this unbalanced situation, the autonomic nervous system attempts to put things in order and the parasympathetic side of the equation jumps in to have its say. The result is a battle ground in the body as the two sides fight to find a new equilibrium. The presenter who has become excited in anticipation of what is about to happen is kept waiting and during this period the parasympathetic side comes into play.

The desire to go to the lavatory, which was previously cut off by the adrenalin released by the sympathetic reaction, is overtaken by the parasympathetic swing and there is sudden need to visit the lavatory, be sick, or feel faint. This is no longer a state of readiness to attack. We can do without these sensations when we are presenting and they must be brought under control.

It is important to control our nerves for three reasons:

■ First, the presenter does not deserve the agony of nerves that are out of control and the humility that is suffered (or thought to be suffered) after a presentation has flopped.

■ Secondly, the audience will react badly to a nervous presenter. The nervousness will transmit; they will find it embarrassing on behalf of the presenter.

■ Finally, the message which is to be imparted will get lost as the presenter's nerves are misconstrued as a sign of a lack of confidence in the findings.

BREATHING

Regaining control of the autonomic nervous system and feeding it with positive stimuli that eclipse the negative reinforcers are not easy and must be addressed at both a physical and mental level. The two are clearly linked. The tension that results in a tightening of the chest, a shortening of breath and loss of control of the voice can be eased by attempting quick relaxation methods. The key to physically regaining control of the nerves just before a presentation is to consciously tense muscles followed by a deliberate and controlled relaxation. This requires concentration and work on a particular muscle group. For example, to relax the chest and get the breathing in order: take a deep breath, hold it for five or six seconds until you feel a self-induced tension. Then, breathe out and concentrate on the feeling of letting go. The tension will disappear and relaxation will follow. So too by tensing and relaxing muscles in the jaw, the neck, the arms and legs, the manifestations of physical stress can be relieved and a feeling of personal control can be reasserted.

YOUR MIND

Behind all the nervous problems of the presenter lies an attitude and mind-set. If it gets out of control, the presenter will go to pieces and could destroy the presentation. The mind will play tricks if it is allowed to do so. Instead of saying that everything will be all right, it reminds us about the difficult questions that might be asked. In the same way it feeds the fear that insufficient is known about the subject to be convincing. If it is allowed to do so, the mind could make the junior researcher think that they are not worthy enough to present to a more senior group of managers.

Wresting control of the mind can be achieved in a number of ways. It can be helpful to think about all the positive reasons why the presentation will go well. You do know your subject, perhaps not perfectly, but then who does? Certainly you know a lot more than most other people and they will be interested to hear what you have to say. By telling yourself that you are knowledgeable and worthy you will demonstrate these qualities to the audience.

Leading on from this, it is a comfort to know that, in the main, people are on the side of the presenter — they want it to be a success for otherwise they will feel embarrassed and that it was a waste of time and money. There could be some 'bash the consultant' types who want to score points or who are playing politics but they are in the minority and in most presentations the rest of the audience will put them down.

There is no need to be intimidated by the audience. Those senior people who seem so terrifying with their fancy titles go home at night and crawl on the carpet with their children or grandchildren and suffer anxieties and self-doubt along with the rest of us. Think of them as ordinary human beings like you, as people who worry and laugh and cry and you will begin to feel differently and far warmer towards them.

THE VOICE AND DELIVERY

During the presentation the voice plays an important role. It is *the* most important communication device and there are a number of points to bear in mind. The first is that the voice carries the presenter's personality and this is to be encouraged as it adds colour and interest. It is wrong to try to cover up a regional accent. To do so would be an extra distraction, which would be something else for the mind to worry and think about. Accents should be allowed to come out and become a feature of the presenter and the presentation. Be yourself but even more so!

During the presentation the delivery of the words will be all the better if you:

■ **Don't mumble.** Speak clearly, face the audience and pace your delivery: 100 words per minute is about right for a presentation as it allows points to sink in and yet it is sufficiently fast to sustain interest. Try a dummy run of the presentation and tape yourself. The adrenalin will not be flowing as it will on the day but the practice will provide a guide as to the speed of delivery and the amount of uhms and ers which are thrown in. Clear speech and diction means facing the audience and spitting out the words from time to time — so remember those in the front row because they will not thank you for a shower.

■ **Don't speak in a monotone.** There is a tendency to let the voice fade and drop off at the end of sentences or after a point has been made. Keep the voice full of pep. Work on underlining your words verbally to emphasise them and avoid slipping into that boring monotone.

■ **Don't repeat the same words.** A common fault of presenters is to go on to auto-pilot and without thinking, a phrase or word is repeated. After the second or third time the phrase is used it will be picked up by the audience who eventually will become irritated or distracted by it. Words and phrases which can easily get

COPING ON THE DAY ■ 121

stuck in the groove are: 'to be honest with you', 'in essence', 'at the end of the day', 'basically', 'essentially'. Use a tape recorder in a practice session or ask friends and colleagues about your own favourite repeats.

APPEARANCE AND DRESS

We dress for occasions. Dress makes us feel good and we would be uncomfortable if we were dressed inappropriately. Most presentations made by researchers span the informal debrief through to a formal presentation to a board. There can be no absolute rules for dress as everyone must do what feels right for themselves. Those who have the personality and flamboyance to carry it off could dress in any way they liked but for most of us, a middle-of-the-road dress code is the norm. Clothes that feel right enable us to eliminate one source of stress and get on with the business in hand, which is concentrating on the presentation. A young researcher presenting to a senior audience would be well advised to dress conservatively in order to enhance their credibility and to avoid the audience being distracted.

Getting the clothes right is just one part of making sure that appearances are as they should be. Other things to remember seem so obvious it is almost insulting to mention them but, from observing some presenters, it would seem that there are still people who need to be reminded to comb their hair and clean their fingernails.

BODY CONTROL

Beyond the voice, the personality is also expressed by body language. While standing in front of an audience the mind is gripped by the intention to move in different directions. It is necessary to stay and give the presentation but there is an understandable desire to cut and run. The body is subjected to conflicting influences that exert pressures in different directions and this can be manifested in unconscious movements —

swaying, pacing up and down, and turning backwards and forwards to and from the screen. According to behavioural psychologists, this is our bodies telling us that we could escape if we wanted to, and with each rhythmic sway or pace we gain a small degree of comfort. The effect can be disastrous with the presenter constantly tripping over the flex of the overhead projector or stepping back and hitting a waste bin or briefcase. It can be helpful to have a video made of yourself giving a presentation and watch these unconscious movements so that they can be controlled if they are too disconcerting.

There is a danger that attempts to control the body result in a rigid, up-tight stance, which causes the presentation to appear wooden in its delivery. As long as body movements are loose and relaxed they will create interest and provide warmth and personality to the presentation. Since the novice presenter is likely to feel anything but relaxed, it is important to keep the body movements in check. Arms flailing and movements that are too exaggerated could become a distraction, not a point of emphasis.

The layout of the room and the table set for the audience should be taken into consideration by presenters as it will influence the limits and scope of their body movement. Some people can only present if the screen is on one side or another; they need a desk or a lectern for their papers. If you are such a person, you should make sure that you have access to the room before the presentation to organise the layout to your preferred position.

Moving up to and within the enclave of the audience also needs careful handling. The presenter who moves from behind the front desk or lectern has taken a great liberty and entered hitherto neutral space. If the desks are laid out in a horseshoe and the presenter walks into the central space, an invasion has been made of the audience's territory, which makes them uneasy. It is an intimate gesture that can work well in training sessions but in a more typical market research presentation it could be considered arrogant and threatening. Similarly, it requires considerable familiarity for a presenter to walk behind any member of the audience as it creates in them a strong feeling of vulnerability and requires them to turn around to see what is happening.

The hands are the most difficult part of the body to control in a presentation. If the nerves are very bad the hands may shake and very evidently so when placing an acetate on the overhead projector. It may be helpful to keep them pressed against the table or out of sight behind the back so that the signs of nervousness do not show. The hands can be used to great effect to stab the air, to bang the table or to gesture, but if managed badly the gestures will look ham-fisted. A pointing stick in the wrong hands can become a conductor's baton and cause the audience's mind to worry about where it will land next. A laser pointing device enables the presenter to point to a screen from quite some distance but the very distance results in so much leverage on the arrow that the slightest wobble of the hand is exaggerated and the nervousness becomes very obvious. Hands stuck into the pockets can appear disrespectful or slovenly. Worse still, they may find coins or keys to jangle.

EYE CONTACT

Facial expressions such as smiling, grimacing and frowning help build character and warmth into the presentation. If they are insincere, the effect will be counterproductive, looking artificial and contrived. Just as important and probably more powerful, is eye contact. The eyes are the means by which we win attention and communicate sincerity. Looking the audience in the eye is an indication of confidence, though to stare at someone too intently would be considered aggressive.

Ten pairs of eyes all staring at the presenter can be intimidating and result in an attempt to escape by gazing into space or looking at the screen. Eye contact needs careful management and control, deliberately sweeping the room and making the whole audience feel included. In normal conversation, eye contact is seldom prolonged and switches back and forth to avoid the intense stare that signals either hostility or considerable intimacy. Sharing eye contact around the room replicates the short gazes that are used in one-to-one conversation. The temptation must be avoided to concentrate on some person who has a friendly smile and nods sympathetically.

When answering questions it is especially relevant to make eye contact with the person who has voiced the query, maintaining the link at the start and the finish of the answer, with others being addressed in the interim. In this way the presenter is establishing communication with *all* the audience, a theme which the reader will recall has been restated time and again throughout this book.

SUMMARY

■

- ■ The key to successful reports and presentations is *clear* communication.
- ■ Different audiences have different needs — tailor the report to the audience.
- ■ Before you start writing, plan the structure of the report carefully.
- ■ As your confidence at reducing mountains of data grows, so will the clarity of your reports.
- ■ The balance between text, tables and graphics will vary from report to report. The structure of the report will depend on
  — the type of research
  — the type of data
  — the expectations of the client.
- ■ A report is *not* a novel.
- ■ Making the report look good *is* important, take time over this.
- ■ To meet the needs of most of the audience develop a flexible presentation.
- ■ Simple presentations are successful presentations.
- ■ Presentations should be short on description and long on interpretation.
- ■ Strong, well chosen, visual aids will make the presentation more memorable, but remember they are there to assist you *not* to dominate the presentation.
- ■ Delivery, appearance and body language require attention for an effective presentation.
- ■ Remember the three rules for good presentations: practice, practice, practice.

INDEX

■